French for Reading and Translation

French for Reading and Translation is a comprehensive introduction to French grammar and vocabulary for those who want to learn to read and understand French, either to conduct academic research or to experience French literature in its original form.

Rather than explaining every grammatical concept in tedious detail, the book gives easy-to-follow explanations followed by abundant examples and opportunities to see the language in use. It encourages readers to learn vocabulary by showing them how to break it down and how to recognize related words. It gives learners the opportunity to use various reading strategies as they apply this newfound knowledge to the French passages provided.

An engaging guide that will help readers decode the intricacies of the French language, this is an ideal resource for graduate students and researchers consulting French sources.

Shannon R. Becker is Assistant Professor of French at Northern Illinois University, USA.

French for Reading and Translation

Shannon R. Becker

Routledge
Taylor & Francis Group
LONDON AND NEW YORK

First published 2021
by Routledge
2 Park Square, Milton Park, Abingdon, Oxon OX14 4RN

and by Routledge
52 Vanderbilt Avenue, New York, NY 10017

Routledge is an imprint of the Taylor & Francis Group, an informa business

British Library Cataloguing-in-Publication Data
A catalogue record for this book is available from the British Library

Library of Congress Cataloging-in-Publication Data
Names: Becker, Shannon R., author.
Title: French for reading and translation / Shannon R. Becker.
Description: 1. | New York : Routledge, 2020. | Includes bibliographical references and index.
Identifiers: LCCN 2020006190 (print) | LCCN 2020006191 (ebook) | ISBN 9780367344559 (hardback) | ISBN 9780367344542 (paperback) | ISBN 9780429325922 (ebook)
Subjects: LCSH: French language—Textbooks for foreign speakers—English. | French language—Readers.
Classification: LCC PC2129.E5 B358 2020 (print) | LCC PC2129.E5 (ebook) | DDC 440—dc23
LC record available at https://lccn.loc.gov/2020006190
LC ebook record available at https://lccn.loc.gov/2020006191

ISBN: 978-0-367-34455-9 (hbk)
ISBN: 978-0-367-34454-2 (pbk)
ISBN: 978-0-429-32592-2 (ebk)

Typeset in Optima
by Apex CoVantage, LLC

To Steve, with all my love

Contents

Acknowledgments

Endless gratitude goes out to my dear friend Matt Valuckis at V as in Victor for his help formatting the images for this textbook. You're the absolute best!

Preface

Learning to read in a second language, whether to conduct research in your field of study, to enhance your professional credentials, or for your own personal fulfillment, is a very different undertaking from learning to speak, listen, or write in that language. Since you are approaching the language with goals other than communication, you have certain advantages. Key among these is the luxury of time – you can take the time you need to process the text and to use reference materials that aid in this endeavor. Importantly, you also have a set of linguistic tools from your native language that you can utilize in conjunction with general analytical skills to help you understand what you are reading in a new language. These aspects help to make second language reading comprehension a very manageable task.

This process does not come without some challenges, however. For instance, reading words without knowing how they should sound can be an uncomfortable feeling, since we tend to "hear" language mentally as we read. Additionally, when the entire vocabulary of a language is new to you, it can be frustrating to stop and look up every word you don't know, making it difficult and time-consuming to get through dense material. In order to build successful second language reading skills, you will need to develop ways of addressing these issues as well.

In *French for Reading and Translation*, rather than overload you with endless lists of vocabulary that require rote memorization and tedious grammar rules with countless exceptions, I explain the grammatical concepts in clear and concise language accompanied by plentiful examples, give you the strategies you need to break down French vocabulary and sentence structure, and lead you through a range of activities to put that knowledge to use. The following features are important innovations of this textbook:

- **Reading strategies.** In the preliminary chapter I provide you with several reading strategies that can be applied to the texts throughout the book (and beyond). Additionally, the reading passages in the subsequent chapters come with specific exercises to guide you in noticing language structure and finding important information.
- **Vocabulary breakdown.** Strategies for recognizing cognates are discussed in the preliminary chapter. Each chapter thereafter includes a list of vocabulary essential to the grammatical topic at hand, with additional notes on how this vocabulary is used in everyday language and how to identify similar forms.
- **Varied exercises.** Throughout the book you will be asked to put your knowledge to use through various written exercises. In order to help you analyze and understand the language, these exercises will require different skills each time. You may be asked to choose between two options, to fill in the blank, or to identify a tense, among other tasks. As you develop your skills further, you will be asked to complete reading comprehension and translation exercises.
- **Flexible workbook format.** The overall format of the textbook is designed to guide you quickly and easily through the language, giving you abundant examples and plenty of opportunities to decipher it. *French for Reading and Translation* is a straightforward, easy-to-use workbook that encourages you to discover the language for yourself and gives you the tools to do so.

As you progress through the book, you will work through exercises meant to help you develop an intuitive understanding of what you read. The progression of each chapter leads you from simple to more complex language, using varied activities to solidify knowledge along the way.

- **Funny French!** Every chapter will begin with a short, fun exercise in understanding French humor in order to increase motivation, provide an engaging introduction to the grammatical material for that chapter, and give practice in understanding the gist.
- **Vocabulary.** The vocabulary section will introduce you to verbs, nouns, adverbs, etc., that are pertinent to the main focus of the chapter, all with exercises to help you intuit the meaning of these words and incorporate them into your mental inventory.

- **Grammar.** The grammar section will introduce the main topic of the chapter, with both explanations and important notes about usage, and will give you the opportunity to see and use these structures in action.
- **Reading and translation.** In the reading and translation section, you will be guided in noticing and analyzing the main grammatical concept within a reading passage, using reading strategies to answer open-ended comprehension questions, and translating selected sentences.

It is my goal that once you finish this textbook, no matter what your purpose for learning the language, you will feel comfortable reading a wide variety of text types in French. You will have a strong grasp of the structure of its words and sentences, and be able to make educated guesses about unfamiliar words and expressions based on this knowledge. I hope you will be able to make use of these new skills to achieve your personal and professional goals and, who knows, maybe you'll even decide you want to learn how to speak French!

Preliminary chapter

Reading strategies, cognates, and pronunciation

Since you are (presumably) starting from square one in learning to read French, you are going to have a learning curve, and that's totally understandable. Especially where reading is concerned, it's going to take some time before you are able to casually skim a text and comprehend all of it. It is my intention that this chapter provide you with the tools you need to start this journey as well as those you can apply later on as your reading ability improves.

I. Introduction to reading strategies

Reading involves a complicated interaction of what we call bottom-up and top-down cognitive processes. Bottom-up processes involve starting at the smallest units of meaning and working your way up. This includes things such as recognizing words and understanding how they relate to each other within the structure of a sentence. As you might have guessed, then, top-down processes go in the other direction – for example, understanding the overall gist of a text or applying your own background knowledge to further your comprehension.

Both types of processing are important for reading, and they work in tandem, but research has shown that beginners have a hard time applying top-down processes to their reading until they've reached a certain threshold of language knowledge. This makes sense – when you're busy looking up all the words in a text and trying to decide whether they're nouns or verbs, you're going to have a hard time concentrating on the overall meaning.

It makes sense then for you to start by using strategies that rely on bottom-up processing. That's why in the beginning we'll concentrate on recognizing words based on endings and placement; scanning to find words you know;

using contextual clues to make guesses about meaning, etc. At this point you'll find it helpful to have a French-English dictionary or online reference handy to look up words you don't know. Here are some strategies to help you navigate this phase:

- Use word endings to help you identify words and their grammatical categories.
- Find words you already know to use as guideposts in understanding the sentence.
- Scan the text for cognates to add to what you already know.
- Train yourself to recognize chunks of language as you learn them, like subject/verb combinations, prepositional phrases, relative clauses, etc.

As you progress through the book and in your outside readings, you can and should start applying top-down strategies. These can include applying background knowledge about the topic; activating schemata; and skimming the text to find specific information. You should:

- Skim the text for key words and phrases to help determine the topic.
- Use what you already know about that topic to help guess the meaning of expressions with which you may still be unfamiliar.
- Recognize more complicated grammatical constructions and how they're used.

II. Cognates and *faux amis*

One of the best things about reading French is that there is a wealth of cognates. Cognates are words that share a common etymological origin. This can mean that they descended from a common parent language, or that they've been directly borrowed from another language. The technical definition of a cognate can be complicated, so for our purposes we'll rely on how the term is typically used in language learning: to refer to words that look alike in both languages.

You may have already noticed, for example, that a lot of *-tion* and *-sion* words are identical in French and English: *nation, éducation, condition, introduction, communication, passion, obsession, conclusion,* etc. Others may have slight spelling differences but will otherwise be easy to decipher: *dictionnaire, chocolat, dentiste, vanille,* and *famille,* for example. There are many great resources on the Internet where you can find long lists of French-English cognates, and you should absolutely take some time to find and study them.

Mais attention! Things can never be too easy – sometimes you'll come across a word that seems to be a cognate, but that has different meanings in the two languages. As we progress through the chapters together, I'll point out some of these *faux amis* (false friends). But we may as well start by looking at a short list of the most common ones.

French word	Real meaning	Wrong meaning	That word in French
actuellement	currently	actually	*en fait*
assister à	to attend	to assist	*aider*
attendre	to wait for	to attend	*assister à*
avertissement	warning	advertisement	*publicité*
blesser	to injure/hurt	to bless	*bénir*
demander	to ask	to demand	*exiger*
formidable	great/terrific	formidable	*redoutable*
librairie	bookstore	library	*bibliothèque*
rester	to stay	to rest	*se reposer*
sensible	sensitive	sensible	*raisonnable*
travailler	to work	to travel	*voyager*

Aside from memorizing these and other *faux amis,* you're most likely to learn them through experience and making mistakes. As you're reading a text, if you naturally translate a word into English that seems bizarre, stop and look it up to find out whether it might be a false friend. It probably is, and now you'll be more likely to remember that word when you come across it in future readings.

III. French pronunciation and spelling

For most second language learners, knowledge of pronunciation is important in learning how to recognize words. This may seem counterintuitive, but it relates back to what I mentioned in the preface about how we tend to hear language as we read it. After all, in our native language we learn how to say a word long before we learn how to read it, so once we do learn to read, we've encoded both types of information for that word in our brain. Not having this knowledge can make learning to read in another language feel strange and difficult. That's why you'll see occasional notes on pronunciation throughout the book, and it's also why I'm giving you a few tips here.

- Consonants at the end of words are rarely pronounced.
  - e.g. *petit* and *grand* end in vowel sounds
- If the letter -*e*- is added after a consonant, that consonant will then be pronounced.
  - e.g. *petite* and *grande* end in consonant sounds
- If a word ends in an unaccented -*e*-, the -*e*- is not pronounced.
  - e.g. *dentiste, triste, forme, lourde* end in consonant sounds
- If a word ends in an accented -*é*-, then it is pronounced.
  - e.g. *cliché, café, été* end in vowel sounds
- In order to avoid having two vowels next to each other, elision occurs in small words:
  - e.g. *je* + *aime* = *j'aime, le* + article = *l'article, te* + *appelle* = *t'appelle*
- The letter -*h*- is never pronounced at the beginning of words.
- French has nasal vowels, and they're found in front of the nasal consonants -*m*- and -*n*-.
  - e.g. *v**in**, p**ain**, b**ain**, **tem**ps, **en**tre, m**on**, **son*** end in nasal vowel sounds
- When the letter -*c*- is accented with a *cédille*, -*ç*-, it is pronounced like an -*s*-.
  - e.g. *garçon, façon, leçon*

As you complete the reading and translation activities in this book, keep in mind these reading strategies, cognates, and pronunciation tips. You can always refer back to them as you go along. *Bon courage!*

1 Nouns, articles, and prepositions

I. Funny French!

To start: How many of the nouns (under the fish) can you recognize as cognates? Given these, do you have any guesses about the meaning of the other nouns? Can you decipher the last noun based on the position of the fish?

Pour vous aider à bien comprendre votre poisson rouge

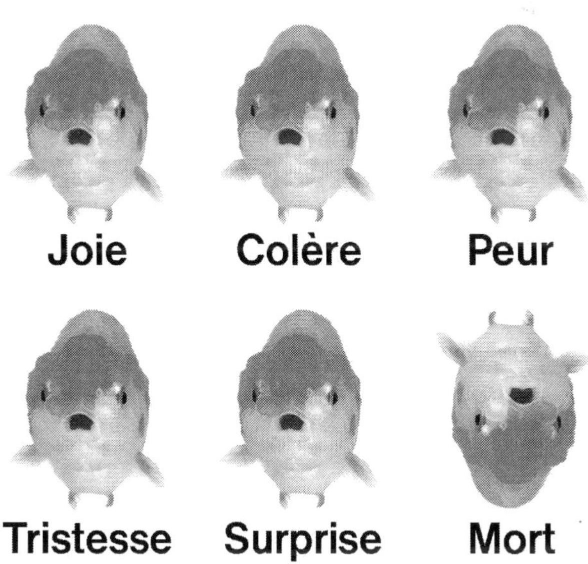

Verify: Now, what do you think the caption says? Which words might mean "goldfish"? Go ahead and look up the remaining words to make sure you've correctly understood the joke.

II. Vocabulary

Look through this list of some common French nouns. In the Grammar section that follows, we will explore the concepts of gender, number, and articles, but for now it will suffice to become familiar with a few of the words you are likely to encounter in French texts. As you go through the list, notice how many of the words are cognates.

un âge	an age
un arbre	a tree
un avion	a plane
un chapeau	a hat
une chose	a thing
une école	a school
une église	a church
un endroit	a place
un exemple	an example
une expression	an expression
une femme	a woman
une fille	a girl
une fleur	a flower
un garçon	a boy
une histoire	a story
un homme	a man
un journal	a newspaper
un livre	a book
un médecin	a doctor
une nation	a nation
un ordinateur	a computer
un pays	a country
un problème	a problem
un professeur	a teacher
un sentiment	a feeling

un stylo a pen
une table a table
une ville a city

Work with it

A. Complete the following sentences with the most logical noun from the list above.

1. Fatigué, il cherche un ________________ pour dormir.

2. Dans le cours de littérature, nous lisons un ________________ très intéressant.

3. Chaque soir elles dînent ensemble à la________________.

4. Le matin, j'aime lire le ________________ en buvant mon café.

5. Puisqu'ils sont pieux, ils cherchent une ________________ à fréquenter.

B. Using what you may already know about French, in addition to the examples you see above, try to identify and underline all the nouns in the following dialogue, from *Entre Nous* by Lucie Vos (1906).

Jean va à la cuisine. Il a mis le chapeau de son Papa.

Rose, la bonne, est en train de peler des pommes.

"Tiens, tiens," dit-elle, "quel est ce monsieur qui entre dans ma cuisine?"

"Je suis le docteur," dit Jean.

"Ah! ah! vous êtes le docteur? Et monsieur le docteur vient peut-être chercher une pomme?"

"Non, Rose, je ne viens pas chercher une pomme, mais un bout de ficelle."

"Un bout de ficelle, pourquoi faire?"

"Pour réparer Paul."

"Tiens, Paul s'est donc cassé le bras? Est-il tombé?"

"Oui, Rose, il est tombé de la table. Je suis le docteur et je le guérirai, ce pauvre petit blessé. Mais c'est bien difficile. Avez-vous un bout de ficelle?"

III. Grammar

A. Gender and number

Gender: As in many languages, nouns in French are marked with a grammatical gender, either masculine or feminine. Since gender is a grammatical construct, you'll find that it usually feels arbitrary. It's usually unrelated to the nature of the noun itself, although certain nouns that refer to people will match the gender of the person. For example, the words for "mother" and "sister" are feminine and the words for "father" and "brother" are masculine. A few other nouns can change gender depending on the actual person to whom you are referring. For example, the word *ami* (friend) can be masculine or feminine (*un ami/une amie*).

As you learn more nouns, it will help to learn the article along with them. This way, you'll associate the noun with its gender and you'll develop an intuition for what "sounds right." This isn't too important when you're only learning to read French, but it will come in handy if you choose to expand your skills to include speaking and writing.

While there are always exceptions, certain noun endings correlate with one gender or the other. For example, nouns ending in *-age, -al, -eau, -isme,* and *-ment* tend to be masculine, whereas nouns ending in *-ance, -ence, -ette, -sion,* and *-tion* tend to be feminine. The feminine marker *-e* is added to a number of nouns to distinguish them from the masculine form. For example, *ami/amie, cousin/cousine, étudiant/étudiante.*

Number: Number is an easier concept for native English speakers, since many nouns in French are marked as plural by adding the letter *-s*, as in English. Some words, however, are marked as plural with the letter *-x*. These include words whose singular form ends in *-eau, -au, -eu, -ou,* and *-al* or *-ail.* Here are some examples:

	-s		***-x***		***-x***
la table	*les tables*	*le bateau*	*les bateaux*	*le journal*	*les journaux*
le livre	*les livres*	*le genou*	*les genoux*	*le cheval*	*les chevaux*
le jour	*les jours*	*le jeu*	*les jeux*	*le travail*	*les travaux*
la note	*les notes*	*l'eau*	*les eaux*	*l'animal*	*les animaux*

Note: If a French noun already ends in -*s*, -*x*, or -*z*, it does not change in its plural form. We do not add -*es*, for example, like we would in English (e.g. mess → messes).

Work with it

A. In the list of nouns below, take your best guess as to whether it is masculine or feminine by circling the appropriate category, then check the dictionary to verify.

1.	bateau	masc/fem	**4.**	village	masc/fem
2.	fiction	masc/fem	**5.**	cyclisme	masc/fem
3.	étiquette	masc/fem	**6.**	département	masc/fem

B. For the following plural nouns, work backwards to determine their singular form. Use a dictionary or online reference to check your work and to find the meaning of the words.

1.	trous	________	**4.**	manteaux	________
2.	cheveux	________	**5.**	seaux	________
3.	romans	________	**6.**	étudiants	________

B. Articles

Articles belong to a grammatical category called determiners, which always accompany a noun in French. We'll return to this concept in Chapter 4 when we talk about demonstrative and possessive determiners. For now we'll concentrate on three types of determiners: definite, indefinite, and partitive articles.

Articles in French correspond in both gender and number with the noun they describe. For the definite article, rather than only one possibility, like English "the," French has four possibilities. If the noun is singular, you will see either *le*, *la*, or *l'*. *Le* is the masculine form, *la* is the feminine form, and *l'* is used for either gender if the noun that follows starts with a vowel.[1] Plural nouns are easy, since they all use *les*.

Indefinite articles, those that correspond to English "a," "an," or "some," come in three forms: *un* for masculine nouns, *une* for feminine nouns, and *des* for plural nouns.

Here are a few more French nouns to learn, along with their corresponding definite and indefinite articles:

Definite			
Singular		**Plural**	
l'article	the article	*les articles*	the articles
le bureau	the office	*les bureaux*	the offices
le festival	the festival	*les festivals**	the festivals
le mot	the word	*les mots*	the words
l'objectif	the objective	*les objectifs*	the objectives
la personne	the person	*les personnes*	the people
l'université	the university	*les universités*	the universities

*Note that this is an exception to the group of nouns that use -*x* in the plural form.

Indefinite			
Singular		**Plural**	
un article	an article	*des articles*	articles
un bureau	an office	*des bureaux*	offices
un festival	a festival	*des festivals*	festivals
un mot	a word	*des mots*	words
un objectif	an objective	*des objectifs*	objectives
une personne	a person	*des personnes*	people
une université	a university	*des universités*	universities

Partitive articles are used to indicate a quantity of a noun that is uncountable (think soup or flour). These articles can sometimes be difficult for English-speaking learners of French to grasp, because while we may occasionally use the words "some" or "any," we can also drop this determiner altogether (e.g. "I want some pizza" or simply "I want pizza"). This is not possible in French, where you need to use either *du* (masculine), *de la* (feminine), or *des* (plural) to indicate that you want "some" of something. As with the definite article, both the masculine and feminine partitive articles become *de l'* when used in front of a noun that starts with a vowel.

Elle commande toujours **de la** *soupe.*	She always orders soup.
Je veux **du chocolat***!*	I want (some) chocolate!
Du pain*, s'il vous plaît.*	(Some) bread, please.
Voudriez-vous **du vin***?*	Would you like (some) wine?
Je prends **de la tarte aux pommes***.*	I'll take some apple pie.

Note: For partitive articles, if the verb is negated, the article is changed to *de*. For example, in order to negate the second sentence above, I would say *Je ne veux pas de chocolat.*

Work with it

A. In the following sentences, circle the correct definite article based on gender and number.

1. Les étudiants doivent suivre (le/la/l'/les) règles.
2. J'aimerais bien voir (le/la/l'/les) festival ce weekend.
3. (Le/La/L'/Les) objectif est de trouver un poste.
4. Elle a écrit (le/la/l'/les) article dans le journal.
5. On n'aime pas (le/la/l'/les) mots vulgaires.
6. C'est (le/la/l'/les) personne que j'admire.

B. For each of your answers from exercise A, give the corresponding indefinite article (*un, une,* or *des*).

1. ____________ 4. ____________
2. ____________ 5. ____________
3. ____________ 6. ____________

C. Prepositions

The two most common prepositions are *à* ("to" or "at") and *de* ("of" or "from"). It's important to learn about these prepositions along with articles, because in French they form contractions in the masculine and plural forms in the following patterns:

au	*à + le*	*du*	*de + le*
à la	*à + la*	*de la*	*de + la*
aux	*à + les*	*des*	*de + les*

Here are some simple examples of this phenomenon:

Je vais ***au*** *supermarché.*	I'm going **to the** supermarket.
Il pense ***à la*** *nourriture.*	He's thinking **about (the)** food.
Elle répond ***aux*** *lettres.*	She responds **to the** letters.
Que penses-tu ***du*** *résultat?*	What do you think **of the** result?
Nous parlons ***de la*** *musique.*	We are talking **about (the)** music.
Elles ont peur ***des*** *avions.*	They are scared **of** planes.

You might have noticed that contractions with the preposition *de* look just like partitive articles, and you're right. You'll need to pay attention to the context of a reading passage to determine which one is being used.

Work with it

A. Let's go back to the text you saw earlier in the Vocabulary section. This time you should be able to identify the nouns more easily, since you're familiar with the articles and contractions that precede them. Make a list of at least eight nouns with their corresponding article or contraction.

Jean va à la cuisine. Il a mis le chapeau de son Papa.

Rose, la bonne, est en train de peler des pommes.

"Tiens, tiens," dit-elle, "quel est ce monsieur qui entre dans ma cuisine?"

"Je suis le docteur," dit Jean.

"Ah! ah! vous êtes le docteur? Et monsieur le docteur vient peut-être chercher une pomme?"

"Non, Rose, je ne viens pas chercher une pomme, mais un bout de ficelle."

"Un bout de ficelle, pourquoi faire?"

"Pour réparer Paul."

"Tiens, Paul s'est donc cassé le bras? Est-il tombé?"

"Oui, Rose, il est tombé de la table. Je suis le docteur et je le guérirai, ce pauvre petit blessé. Mais c'est bien difficile. Avez-vous un bout de ficelle?"

1. ____________________	**5.** ____________________
2. ____________________	**6.** ____________________
3. ____________________	**7.** ____________________
4. ____________________	**8.** ____________________

B. For each of the following expressions with a contraction and a noun, break down the contraction into its preposition and article, then translate the whole expression into English.

Ex: au supermarché à + le at the supermarket

Expression	**Breakdown**	**Translation**
du jour	__________	__________
des éléments	__________	__________
au centre commercial	__________	__________
aux musées	__________	__________
du comité	__________	__________

C. In the paragraph below, underline the partitive articles. Watch out for cases where it's actually the preposition *de* contracted with a definite article!

Elodie a franchi la porte du restaurant. Assise, elle a commandé du pain avec du beurre avant de se perdre dans un roman. Elle n'a donc pas remarqué quand Paul est arrivé. Il a salué le serveur et s'est assis à la table. Elodie a levé les yeux du roman, contente de voir son ami. Ils ont décidé de prendre du vin et de la quiche lorraine.

IV. Reading and translation

Read the excerpt from *La Maison de Claudine* by Colette (1922) and answer the questions that follow.

> "Il n'y a rien **pour le dîner**, ce soir. . . . Je vais moi-même **à la boucherie**, comme je suis. Quel ennui! Ah! pourquoi mange-t-on? Qu'allons-nous manger ce soir?"
>
> Ma mère est debout, découragée, **devant la fenêtre**. . . . Elle nous regarde, tour à tour, sans espoir. Elle sait qu'aucun de nous ne lui donnera **un avis** utile. Consulté, papa répondra:
>
> "**Des tomates** crues avec **beaucoup de poivre**."
>
> "**Des choux** rouges au vinaigre," eût dit Achille, l'aîné de mes frères, que sa thèse de doctorat retient à Paris.
>
> "**Un** grand **bol** de chocolat!" postulera Léo, le second.

Et je réclamerai, en sautant en l'air parce que j'oublie souvent que j'ai quinze ans passés:

> "**Des pommes de terre** frites! **Des pommes de terre** frites! Et **des noix** avec **du fromage**!"

Mais il paraît que frites, chocolat, tomates et choux rouges ne "font pas un dîner" . . .

> "Pourquoi, maman?"
>
> "Ne pose donc pas **de questions** stupides . . ."

1 Using cognates, as well as what you know so far about nouns and articles, what do you think is the subject of the conversation between the mother and her family?

2 What category do most of the articles highlighted belong to? Definite, indefinite, or partitive? How do you know?

3 Notice that the first three highlighted nouns in the previous text have prepositions in front of them. Translate those three nouns, with their prepositions, on the lines below.

____

____

____

____

Note

1 This is an aspect of French phonology. Two vowels next to each other would necessitate a glottal stop. Instead, the first vowel is deleted in a process called elision.

2 Subjects and verbs, present tense, questions

I. Funny French!

To start: You may already recognize the format of this joke as a humorous depiction of someone forced to choose between two options. To understand further, you'll need to know the words *pote* ("buddy") and *orthographe* ("spelling").

Knowing this, can you identify enough cognates to figure out the meaning of the joke?

Quand ton pote conjugue mal un verbe

To verify: Look up any words that are still giving you trouble, and compare what you've understood with the translation of the joke in the back of the book.

II. Vocabulary

A. Common verbs

Before you learn how verbs are conjugated in French, it will be helpful to become familiar with some of the most common verbs you'll encounter. In this list they appear in their infinitive form. This means they are not conjugated, which is the equivalent of "to + verb" in English. Knowing the various conjugations will allow you to work backward to find the infinitive form of verbs, since this is how they appear in the dictionary.

aller	to go
aimer	to like, to love
arriver	to arrive
attendre	to wait (for)
avoir	to have
connaître	to know
devoir	to have to
dire	to say
donner	to give
entendre	to hear
être	to be
faire	to do
lire	to read
mettre	to put
ouvrir	to open
parler	to speak
partir	to leave
pouvoir	to be able to, can
prendre	to take
rendre	to give back, to return
répondre	to respond
savoir	to know
tenir	to hold, to keep
trouver	to find

venir	to come
vivre	to live
voir	to see
vouloir	to want

Work with it

A. Read the following sentences in English and decide which French infinitive verb would best replace the words in bold.

1. I want **to live** in Montreal some day. ____________________
2. My parents plan **to arrive** in one week. ____________________
3. She loves **to give** gifts. ____________________
4. You have **to open** your book. ____________________
5. They hope **to see** the city. ____________________

B. Now look at the translations of the previous sentences. Circle the infinitive verb and underline the word you think corresponds to the conjugated verb (e.g. "want" in the first sentence).

1. Je veux vivre à Montréal un jour.
2. Mes parents comptent arriver dans une semaine.
3. Elle adore donner des cadeaux.
4. Tu dois ouvrir ton livre.
5. Ils espèrent voir la ville.

B. Avoir *and* faire *expressions*

The verbs *avoir* ("to have") and *faire* ("to do" or "to make") are used in many French expressions. Frequently, phrases that would use the verb "to be" in English use instead *avoir* in French.

avoir chaud	to be hot
avoir de la chance	to be lucky
avoir faim	to be hungry
avoir froid	to be cold
avoir peur de	to be afraid of
avoir raison	to be right

avoir soif	to be thirsty
avoir tort	to be wrong

Faire is also used frequently to talk about everyday activities.

faire attention (*à*)	to pay attention (to)
faire des économies	to save money
faire du shopping	to go shopping
faire face à	to face, to oppose
faire la fête	to party
faire la queue	to wait in line
faire le ménage	to clean the house
faire les courses	to go grocery shopping

Another important use of *faire* is to talk about the weather. You may see the impersonal expression *Il fait . . .* used in the following descriptions of the weather, among others:

Il fait beau	It's nice out
Il fait chaud	It's hot
Il fait du soleil	It's sunny
Il fait du vent	It's windy
Il fait frais	It's chilly
Il fait froid	It's cold
Il fait mauvais	It's bad out
Il fait moche	It's ugly out

Work with it

Decide which *avoir* or *faire* expression is related to the situations below.

1. Saving up to buy a house ________________

2. Seeing a big, mean dog ________________

3. Going outside in the winter ________________

4. Waiting anxiously for your food at a restaurant ________________

5. Getting ready for guests ________________

6. Flying a kite ________________

C. Question words

In the Grammar section, we'll look at how various question words are used in sentences. For now, here is a list of question words, prepositional phrases, and interrogative adjectives that will let you know that what you're reading is indeed a question.

The biggest clue that a question is being asked is the expression *est-ce que,* which can be used alone or in combination with the following words.

Qui	Who	*Pourquoi*	Why
Quoi	What	*Comment*	How
Quand	When	*Combien*	How much/how many
Où	Where		

A quelle heure	At what time
Avec qui	With whom
De quoi	About what

Interrogative adjectives correspond to the English "what" or "which," and make agreement with the nouns that follow them.

quel	which (masculine, singular)
quelle	which (feminine, singular)
quels	which (masculine, plural)
quelles	which (feminine, plural)

Work with it

In these questions, identify the question word, prepositional phrase, or interrogative adjective.

1. Vous aimez qui? ______________________
2. A quelle heure est-ce qu'il arrive? ______________________
3. Avec qui est-ce qu'elles vont au parc? ______________________
4. Où est-ce qu'il habite? ______________________
5. Quelles sont les bonnes réponses? ______________________

III. Grammar

A. *Subject pronouns*

You may or may not recall from English grammar that a pronoun is a word that replaces a noun. There are different types of pronouns, and the first type we'll talk about is the subject pronoun. Here are the French subject pronouns:

je	I	*nous*	we
tu	you (singular)	*vous*	you (plural)
il	he	*ils*	they (masculine)
elle	she	*elles*	they (feminine)
on	one		

There are three points of view: first, second, and third person. *Je* and *nous* are first person, because the speaker is included. *Tu* and *vous* are second person, because they refer to the person or people being addressed. Finally, third person refers to someone who is not part of the conversation, so *il, elle, ils,* or *elles.*

There are three key differences to note between French and English subject pronouns. First, gender is differentiated not only in the third person singular, but in the third person plural as well. Whereas English has "he" and "she" in the singular but only "they" in the plural, French has both *ils* and *elles.* Interestingly, *elles* is only used if a group of people is made up exclusively of women. If even one man is present, the masculine pronoun *ils* is used.

Additionally, there are two French pronouns that equate to "you": *tu* and *vous.* While these denote the difference between singular and plural, they are also used to distinguish between formal and informal address. The informal pronoun *tu* is used for friends, family, and people younger than oneself, while the formal *vous* is used for elders, professional acquaintances, and people one doesn't know.

Finally, the pronoun *on* is used in many more situations than its stuffier sounding English counterpart "one." As you can see in the sentences below, *on* can be used to refer to an entire group of people (1) or to an unknown subject (2). It can also be translated as "you" in English (3), and is frequently used as an informal version of *nous* (4).

On parle français en France.	They speak French in France.
On me téléphone tous les jours.	Someone is calling me every day.
On ne sait jamais.	You never know.
On va à la plage?	Are we going to the beach?

Work with it

Let's work on points of view. Which French subject pronoun is being described?

1. second person plural
2. first person singular
3. third person plural, feminine
4. third person singular, masculine
5. first person plural
6. second person singular
7. third person plural, masculine
8. third person singular, feminine
9. third person singular, impersonal

a. je
b. tu
c. il
d. elle
e. on
f. nous
g. vous
h. ils
i. elles

B. Verb categories

Before you learn the present tense, we need to look briefly at the different categories, or groups, of French verbs, because each group follows certain rules of conjugation. Verbs that follow the pattern of the group they belong to are called regular, and those that follow a different pattern are called irregular. You'll find that there quite a few irregular French verbs.

Broadly, French verbs are divided into three groups[1] based on their ending in the infinitive form, as shown in this table:

-*er* verbs (1st group)		**-*ir* verbs (2nd group)**		**-*re* verbs (3rd group)**	
aimer	to like, love	*choisir*	to choose	*attendre*	to wait
donner	to give	*finir*	to finish	*entendre*	to hear
parler	to speak	*remplir*	to fill	*perdre*	to lose
passer	to pass	*réussir*	to succeed	*rendre*	to give back

There are various exceptions to these groups, including a subset of common verbs that happen to be irregular, the most important of which are *aller, avoir, être,* and *faire.*

As a reader of French, it isn't essential that you know every last exception to the rules of verb conjugation, only that you are able to recognize and break down most verbs. Being familiar with the various possible endings will help you recognize a verb when you see one.

C. Present tense

Use: As opposed to English, where you can express the present tense with either the simple present or the present progressive (e.g. "We eat" or "We are eating"), French uses only the simple present. You must rely on context to determine whether the action being described is habitual or ongoing. For example, *J'écoute de la musique* could mean "I listen to music" or "I'm listening to music."

French is similar to English in that you may find a conjugated verb followed by an infinitive verb, as in the following sentences:

*Elle veut **aller** avec nous.*	She wants **to go** with us.
*Nous préférons **dîner** ensemble.*	We prefer **to eat** together.
*Ils aiment **jouer** au golf.*	They like **to play** golf.

Formation: Regular verbs in the three groups are conjugated by removing the infinitive ending and adding different present tense endings for each subject pronoun, according to the patterns below (with endings highlighted).

1st group: *parl**er***

*je parl**e***	I speak/am speaking	*nous parl**ons***	we speak/are speaking
*tu parl**es***	you speak/are speaking	*vous parl**ez***	you speak/are speaking
*il parl**e***	he speaks/is speaking	*ils parl**ent***	they speak/are speaking
*elle parl**e***	she speaks/is speaking	*elles parl**ent***	they speak/are speaking
*on parl**e***	one speaks/is speaking		

2nd group: *rempl**ir***

*je rempl**is***	I fill/am filling	*nous rempl**issons***	we fill/are filling
*tu rempl**is***	you fill/are filling	*vous rempl**issez***	you fill/are filling
*il rempl**it***	he fills/is filling	*ils rempl**issent***	they fill/are filling
*elle rempl**it***	she fills/is filling	*elles rempl**issent***	they fill/are filling
*on rempl**it***	one fills/is filling		

3rd group: *attend**re***

*j'attend**s***	I wait/am waiting	*nous attend**ons***	we wait/are waiting
*tu attend**s***	you wait/are waiting	*vous attend**ez***	you wait/are waiting
il attend	he waits/is waiting	*ils attend**ent***	they wait/are waiting
elle attend	she waits/is waiting	*elles attend**ent***	they wait/are waiting
on attend	one waits/is waiting		

Here are the conjugations for *aller, avoir, être,* and *faire,* since not only will we be analyzing these verbs in the next section, but they are also incredibly common.

avoir		***être***	
j'ai	*nous avons*	*je suis*	*nous sommes*
tu as	*vous avez*	*tu es*	*vous êtes*
il/elle/on a	*ils/elles ont*	*il/elle/on est*	*ils/elles sont*
aller		***faire***	
je vais	*nous allons*	*je fais*	*nous faisons*
tu vas	*vous allez*	*tu fais*	*vous faites*
il/elle/on va	*ils/elles vont*	*il/elle/on fait*	*ils/elles font*

Work with it

A. In the following sentences, underline the subject pronoun and circle the conjugated verb.

1. Nous aimons voyager.
2. Il va souvent chez sa grand-mère.
3. Vous prenez du thé?
4. Ils choisissent un cadeau.
5. Elle remplit son verre.
6. Tu fais tes exercices?

B. For the sentences in exercise A, work backward to find the infinitive form of the conjugated verbs.

1. ________________ **4.** ________________
2. ________________ **5.** ________________
3. ________________ **6.** ________________

D. Negation

Basic negation in French requires two small words, *ne* and *pas,* placed on either side of the conjugated verb. Here a few simple examples:

Il ***n'****étudie* ***pas****.*	He does **not** study/is not studying.
Nous ***ne*** *sommes* ***pas*** *fatigués.*	We are **not** tired.
Vous ***n'****allez* ***pas*** *au concert?*	You're **not** going to the concert?
Je ***ne*** *sors* ***pas*** *souvent.*	I do**n't** go out often.
Elles ***ne*** *voyagent* ***pas*** *cette année.*	They are**n't** traveling this year.

Notice that not all of these examples are translated by the present progressive in English. For instance, it would seem strange to say "We are being tired" or "I'm not going out often." With more practice, it will become intuitive to translate the French simple present into whichever English form makes most sense in the context of the larger passage.

Pronunciation note: The word *ne* undergoes the process of elision, where a sound is omitted along with its corresponding letter in the spelling. In this case, since *ne* is followed by a vowel in the first and third examples, it is changed to *n'* to reflect the pronunciation.

Negation doesn't always take the form *ne . . . pas,* which corresponds to "not." You may also encounter other forms of negation, corresponding to "never," "no one," "nothing," etc. Just like *ne . . . pas,* these expressions are made up of two words that go around a conjugated verb.

Here are some of the most common negative expressions:

ne . . . aucun	none, not any
ne . . . jamais	never
ne . . . pas du tout	not at all
ne . . . pas encore	not yet
ne . . . pas non plus	not . . . either
ne . . . personne	no one
ne . . . plus	not anymore, no longer, no more
ne . . . point	not (literary)
ne . . . que	only
ne . . . rien	nothing

As you read the following sample sentences, think about how the meaning would change if *ne . . . pas* were used instead.

Tu ***ne*** *fais* ***jamais*** *de sport.*	You **never** work out.
Je ***ne*** *chante* ***plus****.*	I do**n't** sing **anymore**.
Il ***ne*** *dit* ***rien****.*	He does**n't** say **anything**/He says **nothing**.
Nous ***ne*** *voyons* ***personne****.*	We do**n't** see **anyone**/We see **no one**.
Elles ***n'****ont* ***aucune*** *idée.*	They have **no** idea.
Je ***n'****aime* ***pas du tout*** *ce cours.*	I do**n't** like this class **at all**.
Vous ***ne*** *mangez* ***que*** *des légumes.*	You **only** eat vegetables.

Importantly, although *rien* and *personne* are direct objects in these examples, they can also function as the subject of a sentence. When this happens, the word order is reversed:

Personne n'*aime les maths.*	**No one** likes math.
Rien ne *se passe.*	**Nothing** is happening.

Work with it

A. In this paragraph, find the verbs that are negated and underline them (including the *ne* and the *pas*).

Mon frère est mon meilleur ami. Par contre nous n'aimons pas toujours faire la même chose. Je sors souvent sans lui, parce qu'il n'est pas aussi sociable que moi. Il aime rester à la maison, où il regarde la télé et écoute de la musique. Je préfère être avec mes amis, mais je n'ai pas beaucoup d'argent donc parfois je ne peux pas sortir. Ces jours-là, j'adore passer du temps avec mon frère à discuter de tout et de rien.

B. Based on context, circle the word(s) that best complete(s) the sentence. Look up words as necessary, and use what you've learned about infinitives to find the verbs you don't know. Then write out the equivalent negative expression in English.

1. Nous ne travaillons (rien/pas du tout). ____________________
2. Je ne joue (personne/jamais) au football. ____________________
3. Il ne voit (rien/jamais) sans lunettes. ____________________
4. Nous ne mangeons (plus/aucun) dessert. ____________________
5. Elles ne détestent (personne/pas du tout). ____________________
6. Tu n'es (jamais/plus) professeur? ____________________

E. *Question formation*

There are a few ways to form a question in French. As a reader, you have the luxury of the question mark to clue you in, but I'll introduce you to some additional visual cues you may encounter. These are key words (question words, prepositional phrases, and interrogative adjectives), subject-verb inversion, and the expressions *est-ce que* and *n'est-ce pas*.

The expression *est-ce que* literally means "is it that." When placed in front of a sentence, *est-ce que* transforms a statement into a yes/no question. For example:

Tu as froid.	You are cold.	***Est-ce que*** *tu as froid?*	Are you cold?
Il est méchant.	He is mean.	***Est-ce qu'****il est méchant?*	Is he mean?
Vous sortez.	You're going out.	***Est-ce que*** *vous sortez?*	Are you going out?

Sometimes learners get hung up on the literal meaning of *est-ce que* and find it confusing. It might be helpful for you to get into the habit of processing it as one word, and thinking of it as a simple visual signal that what you're reading is a question.

Another easy way to recognize a question is through question words, like those introduced in the Vocabulary section. As a reminder, the basic question words in French are:

Qui	Who	*Pourquoi*	Why
Quoi	What	*Comment*	How
Quand	When	*Combien*	How much/how many
Où	Where		

Note: When used at the start of a question, the word *quoi* becomes *que*. The process of elision then turns this into *qu'* in front of the expression *est-ce que*, which gives us *qu'est-ce que*.

You may also see prepositional phrases used as question words, such as:

A quelle heure	At what time
Avec qui	With whom
De quoi	About what

Finally, you may see interrogative adjectives used in conjunction with nouns at the beginning or end of a question. Note that these words can be translated into English as either "what" or "which."

Quel *est ton nom de famille?*	**What** is your last name?
Quelle *est ton émission de télé préférée?*	**What** is your favorite TV show?
Vous avez choisi ***quels*** *plats?*	**Which** dishes have you chosen?
Quelles *idées sont les meilleures?*	**Which** ideas are the best?

Question words can be used along with the expression *est-ce que*, but it is not required. If they are used with *est-ce que*, they appear at the beginning of the sentence. If they are used without *est-ce que*, they go at the end of the sentence.

Quand *est-ce qu'ils partent?* *Ils partent* ***quand****?*	When are they leaving?
Où *est-ce qu'il va?* *Il va* ***où****?*	Where is he going?
A quelle heure *est-ce que tu sors?* *Tu sors* ***à quelle heure****?*	What time are you going out?
Quand *est-ce qu'elle rentre?* *Elle rentre* ***quand****?*	When is she coming home?

Another possible question format is subject-verb inversion. Questions are formed this way in English as well, though they're complicated by the auxiliary verb "do." French is simpler in this regard, since only one verb is used. Look at this list of sentences and reflect on the differences between French and English.

Préférez-vous *le vin rouge ou blanc?*	**Do you prefer** red or white wine?
Aimes-tu *cette pièce de théâtre?*	**Do you like** this play?
A-t-il[2] *assez d'argent?*	**Does he have** enough money?
Jouent-elles *du piano?*	**Do they play** piano?
As-tu *du temps libre?*	**Do you have** some free time?

Finally, you may come across a statement with the tag *n'est-ce pas* (literal meaning: "is it not") added as a request for confirmation. This would usually be translated as "right?" in English.

Vous êtes professeur, **n'est-ce pas**?	You're a teacher, right?
Il vient avec nous, **n'est-ce pas**?	He's coming with us, right?
Elles prennent du thé, **n'est-ce pas**?	They're having tea, right?

Work with it

A. Take the following statements and transform them into questions using the format given.

Ex: Ils vont à la bibliothèque. → Est-ce qu'ils vont à la bibliothèque? (est-ce que)

1. Elle est biologiste. (n'est-ce pas) ____________________

2. Tu connais mon frère. (inversion) ____________________

3. Ils adoptent un chien. (est-ce que) ____________________

4. Il a peur des abeilles. (est-ce que) ____________________

5. Vous répondez aux questions. (inversion) ____________________

B. Based on the context in the sentence(s), fill in the appropriate question word or interrogative adjective from the choices in the box.

quoi (qu')	qui	comment	où	pourquoi	quand	quel
quelle	quels	quelles				

1. ________ est-ce que tu vas pour trouver des fraises?

2. Quand vous cuisinez, ________est-ce que vous faites?

3. ________ est ta nationalité? Je suis américaine.

4. Avec ________ est-ce qu'elle va au cinéma?

5. Tu chantes très bien. ________ as-tu appris à chanter comme ça?

6. Je ne comprends pas. ________ est-ce qu'il aime cette fille?

7. Je ne peux pas choisir. ________ voiture préfères-tu?

8. J'y vais demain. ________ allez-vous?

IV. Reading and translation

Scan the following excerpt from *Les caves du Vatican* by André Gide (1912), and answer the questions below.

> "Qu'est-ce que c'est que ces machinettes-là?"

Julie comprend fort bien que la question n'est pas sérieuse; mais pourquoi s'offusquerait-elle?

> "Comment, mon oncle! Vous n'avez jamais vu des médailles?"
> "Ma foi non, ma petite," ment-il; "**ça n'est pas joli-joli, mais je pense que cela sert à quelque chose**."

Et comme la sereine piété ne répugne pas à quelque espièglerie innocente, l'enfant avise, contre la glace au-dessus de la cheminée, une photographie qui la représente et, la désignant du doigt:

> "Vous avez là, mon oncle, le portrait d'une petite fille qui n'est pas non plus joli-joli. **A quoi donc peut-il vous servir**?"

1 How many present tense subject/verb combinations can you find? How many questions? How many negative constructions?

2 Can you translate the phrases highlighted in bold? Use a dictionary for the words you don't know, and check your answers in the back of the book. (***Hint***: Look up "servir à" together.)

____

____

____

____

Notes

1 Grammarians have different ways of categorizing French verbs. This is the most common way, but there is not a consensus on the best way since there are so many exceptions.

2 The *-t-* in *a-t-il* has no grammatical or lexical function. Rather, it's another way to avoid having two vowel sounds next to each other.

3 Adjectives and adverbs

I. Funny French!

To start: This should be an easy one. Have you heard the repeated sentence before? In the words underneath the conversation, how many cognates do you see?

Ça va?
Ça va. Ça va?
Ça va.

Une conversation
française traditionnelle.

Verify: Check the meaning in the back. Identify the two adjectives and compare their positions in French and English. We'll be looking more closely at adjectives in this chapter.

II. Vocabulary

A. Common adjectives

There are two important clues for recognizing adjectives: agreement and position. We'll delve more deeply into those aspects in the Grammar section;

for now, let's look at some common French adjectives. Where applicable, they are listed with the masculine and feminine forms.

ancien/ancienne	old
autre	other
beau/belle	beautiful
bon/bonne	good
certain/certaine	certain
content/contente	happy
dernier/dernière	last
différent/différente	different
difficile	difficult
entier/entière	entire/whole
étrange	strange
faux/fausse	false, fake
facile	easy
faible	weak
fatigué/fatiguée	tired
gentil/gentille	nice, kind
grand/grande	big, tall
important/importante	important
intelligent/intelligente	intelligent
lent/lente	slow
libre	free
mauvais/mauvaise	bad
même	same
nouveau/nouvelle	new
petit/petite	small, short
possible	possible
prêt/prête	ready
prochain/prochaine	next
sympa(thique)	nice, kind
triste	sad
vite	fast
vrai/vraie	true

Look back through the list and notice that most, though not all, adjectives follow the pattern of adding the letter *-e* for the feminine form.

Another thing you can notice at this point is that there are many cognates in this list: *important, intelligent, différent,* and *certain* are just a few examples.

Work with it

Match the French adjectives on the left to their English equivalents on the right. While some of these are from the list above, I have also included new ones to test your skills.

1. certain/certaine	**a.** false, fake
2. libre	**b.** certain
3. âgé/âgée	**c.** good
4. délicieux/délicieuse	**d.** free
5. prêt/prête	**e.** fat
6. faux/fausse	**f.** ready
7. gros/grosse	**g.** old
8. bon/bonne	**h.** delicious

B. Common adverbs

Many French adverbs are recognizable by their ending, *-ment,* which is equivalent to the *-ly* of English. This ending is added to the feminine form of the adjective, in the following pattern:

lent (masc)	→ *lente* (fem)	→ *lentement*	slowly
certain (masc)	→ *certaine* (fem)	→ *certainement*	certainly
entier (masc)	→ *entière* (fem)	→ *entièrement*	entirely

Not all adverbs follow this exact pattern, and there are several irregular adverbs that do their own thing. We'll break those down further in the

Grammar section, but for now let's look at some common adverbs you're likely to come across in your reading. Some have the *-ment* ending, but many do not.

absolument	absolutely
actuellement	currently
alors	so, well, then
ainsi	thus, so
après	after(ward)
assez	enough
avant	before
avec	with
beaucoup	a lot
bien	well
cependant	however
comme	as
davantage	more
depuis	since
désormais	from now on
encore	still, yet
heureusement	fortunately
ici	here
immédiatement	immediately
là-bas	there
mal	poorly
parfois	sometimes
partout	everywhere
plutôt	rather
pourquoi	why
puis	then
seulement	only
souvent	often
surtout	especially
tant	so much
tellement	so much
toujours	always
trop	too (much)
vraiment	really, truly

Work with it

Fill in the missing steps in the table showing the change from adjectives to adverbs, following the example in the top row.

lent	**lente**	**lentement**
immédiat		immédiatement
	actuelle	actuellement
tel	telle	
seul		seulement
heureux	heureuse	
	généreuse	généreusement

III. Grammar

A. *Adjectives*

Agreement: Just as determiners such as definite and indefinite articles agree in gender and number with the noun they accompany, so do adjectives. In the Vocabulary section, you saw that for many adjectives, this agreement means adding the letter *-e* to make it feminine. Some of these adjectives may also undergo slight spelling changes, like an accent on the second to last vowel (see words marked with an asterisk).

certain/certaine	certain
content/contente	happy
*dernier/dernière**	last
*entier/entière**	entire
fatigué/fatiguée	tired
grand/grande	big, tall
important/importante	important
lent/lente	slow

mauvais/mauvaise	bad
petit/petite	small, short
*premier/première**	first
vrai/vraie	true

For some adjectives, an extra consonant is added to the masculine form before adding -*e*:

ancien/ancienne	old
bon/bonne	good
gentil/gentille	nice, kind
gros/grosse	fat

Moreover, other adjectives undergo bigger changes from the masculine to the feminine form:

beau/belle	beautiful
doux/douce	gentle, sweet
faux/fausse	false, fake
heureux/heureuse	happy
nouveau/nouvelle	new
sérieux/sérieuse	serious
travailleur/travailleuse	hardworking
vieux/vieille	old

Finally, some adjectives don't change at all from the masculine to the feminine form. This is because they already end in -*e*. Only those that end in an accented -*é* require an additional -*e*. For example, *fatigué, énervé,* and *animé* become *fatiguée, énervée,* and *animée*. However, the following adjectives look the same in both forms:

autre	other	*jeune*	young
bizarre	bizarre	*libre*	free
difficile	difficult	*même*	same
drôle	funny	*possible*	possible
facile	easy	*rare*	rare
faible	weak	*triste*	sad

Adjectives also agree in number with their noun (i.e. singular or plural). For many of them, this means adding *-s* just as in English. However, much like the nouns you saw in Chapter 1, some adjectives end in *-x* when they're plural. The plural form may also look different depending on whether it's masculine or feminine. As you look through the following list of singular and plural adjectives, note the differences.

Singular masculine	Singular feminine	Plural masculine	Plural feminine
âgé	*âgée*	*âgés*	*âgées*
bon	*bonne*	*bons*	*bonnes*
certain	*certaine*	*certains*	*certaines*
dernier	*dernière*	*derniers*	*dernières*
gros	*grosse*	*gros*	*grosses*
heureux	*heureuse*	*heureux*	*heureuses*
triste	*triste*	*tristes*	*tristes*

Placement: Contrary to English, most French adjectives are placed after the noun they modify.

des filles travailleuses hardworking girls
un garçon sérieux a serious boy
une réunion importante an important meeting
des biscuits délicieux delicious cookies
un cours intéressant an interesting class

There are two exceptions to this placement rule. The first is a subgroup of adjectives that describe beauty, age, goodness, and size (frequently taught using the acronym BAGS).

une jolie femme a pretty woman
un bon film a good movie
la première année the first year
une nouvelle voiture a new car
un gros câlin a big hug

Another subset of adjectives can go either before **or** after the noun, and have a different meaning depending on the position. These include, but aren't limited to, the words: *ancien, cher, grand, pauvre,* and *propre*. Look at the examples below to see the differences in meaning:

un grand homme	a great man	*un homme grand*	a tall man
la pauvre femme	the poor woman	*la femme pauvre*	the poor woman (not rich)
un ancien collègue	an ex-colleague	*un collègue ancien*	an old colleague (age)
ma propre chambre	my own room	*ma chambre propre*	my clean room

Work with it

A. Using contextual cues (e.g. articles, subjects), circle the correct form of the adjective.

1. Mon ami a acheté une [gros/grosse] voiture.
2. Elle a fait le [mauvais/mauvaise] choix.
3. Le petit chien est très [fatigué/fatiguée] après la promenade.
4. J'écris une [nouveau/nouvelle] pièce de théâtre.
5. Il est tellement [heureux/heureuse] d'être là.
6. La phrase que je lis est [vrai/vraie].

B. For each of the sentences below, circle all of the adjectives you can identify.

1. L'enfant voit un grand ballon rouge.
2. Elle achète une petite maison propre avec un joli jardin.
3. Il veut un certain chemisier qu'il a vu dans la nouvelle boutique du coin.
4. Le petit garçon est triste parce qu'il a perdu sa belle poupée.
5. Nous passons la journée entière à parler des choses drôles.
6. La pauvre vieille femme ne réussit pas à trouver de nouveaux vêtements.

B. Adverbs

Formation: We looked at the basic formation of adverbs in the Vocabulary section, which you'll recall involves taking the feminine form of the adjective and adding *-ment*. In the list above, there were quite a few adverbs that didn't take this form at all, many of which have to do with either time or place (e.g. *ici, avant, après, là-bas, encore*, etc.). There is also a subset of adjectives that change their spelling considerably when transformed into adverbs. These are adjectives that end in either *-ant* or *-ent*, which follow the pattern below:

violent	→ violemment	élégant	→ élégamment
fréquent	→ fréquemment	courant	→ couramment
évident	→ évidemment	brillant	→ brillamment
patient	→ patiemment	abondant	→ abondamment

Adjectives that end in a vowel do not need to take the feminine form before adding *-ment*. Additionally, some adjectives that end in *-e* add an accent to that vowel before the *-ment*.

absolu	→ absolument	profond/profonde	→ profondément
poli	→ poliment	énorme	→ énormément
vrai	→ vraiment	précis/précise	→ précisément

There are two adverbs that work much the same as they do in English, in that they are different from their adjectival counterparts. These are *bien* (well) and *mal* (poorly), which correspond to the adjectives *bon* (*bonne, bons, bonnes*) and *mauvais* (*mauvaise, mauvaises*), respectively.

Placement: Adverbs follow stricter rules of placement in French than in English. Typically, a French adverb will go directly after the conjugated verb that it modifies.

Elle chante ***bien***.	She sings well.
Nous regardons ***souvent*** *la télé.*	We watch TV often.
Tu es ***actuellement*** *en route?*	You're currently on the way?
Il mange ***beaucoup***.	He eats a lot.
Je rentre ***immédiatement***.	I'm going back immediately.

Note that in these examples the verbs are in the present tense. In the next chapter you'll learn about the imperfect and the compound past. Adverbs will follow the same rule in the past tense, generally following right after a conjugated verb. More on that later!

Work with it

A. In the list below, circle all the words that are adverbs.

certain	entièrement	souvent	mauvais
tellement	ainsi	facile	nouvelle
encore	toujours	libre	joliment
énorme	bien	évidemment	trop
beaucoup	assez	âgée	rarement
après	vraiment	dernier	seul

B. In the following sentences, circle the adverb and draw an arrow to the word that it modifies (***Hint***: This could be a verb, an adjective, or another adverb). Then on the right, give the English word for the adverb.

1. Ils voient souvent leur grand-mère. ____________________
2. Ces chiens sont très mignons. ____________________
3. Il fait trop beau aujourd'hui. ____________________
4. Tu es vraiment méchant. ____________________
5. Elle parle trop sans réfléchir. ____________________

C. Comparatives and superlatives

Comparing adjectives: Comparing adjectives is relatively simple in French, and follows the pattern shown here:

plus (more)				
moins (less)	+	adjective	+	*que* (than)
aussi (as)				

This will give you a construction that is equivalent to the following expressions in English:

plus intelligent que	smarter (more intelligent) than
moins intelligent que	less intelligent than
aussi intelligent que	as intelligent as

Let's look at a few sample sentences:

*Elle est **plus intelligente que** son frère.*	She is **smarter than** her brother.
*Je suis **moins enthousiaste que** toi.*	I am **less enthusiastic than** you.
*Nous sommes **aussi contents que** nos amis.*	We are **as happy as** our friends.

The adjectives *bon* (*bonne, bons, bonnes*) and *mauvais* (*mauvaise, mauvaises*), or "good" and "bad," have irregular forms in the comparative construction, according to the following pattern:

	Singular (masc.)	Singular (fem.)	Plural (masc.)	Plural (fem.)
bon	*meilleur*	*meilleure*	*meilleurs*	*meilleures*
mauvais	*pire/plus mauvais*	*pire/plus mauvaise*	*pires/plus mauvais*	*pires/plus mauvaises*

Meilleur and *pire* correspond to the English "better" and "worse." Much as in English, they don't necessarily include an explicit comparison, but can stand on their own. Note that *pire* is used more frequently than *plus mauvais*, which has recently become acceptable, but that *pis* is also possible, especially in literary contexts.

*Mes nouvelles chaussures sont **meilleures**.*	My new shoes are **better**.
*C'est **un meilleur livre que** l'autre.*	It's **a better book than** the other one.
*Cette émission est **pire** maintenant.*	This (TV) show is **worse** now.
*Tes amis sont **plus mauvais que** les miens.*	Your friends are **worse than** mine.
*Ça va de mal en **pis**.*	It's going from bad to **worse**.

Work with it

Read the following sentences, underline the adjective, and then break down what is being compared and how, using the format and model given.

1. Mes parents sont moins stricts que mes grands-parents.
2. Les chats sont plus indépendants que les chiens.
3. Les femmes sont aussi intelligentes que les hommes.
4. Elle est plus détendue que son frère.
5. Je suis beaucoup moins enthousiaste que mon père.

	Thing 1	+ – =	Thing 2
1.	Mes parents	–	Mes grands-parents
2.	________	________	________
3.	________	________	________
4.	________	________	________
5.	________	________	________

Comparing adverbs: Adverbs follow the same construction as adjectives in the comparative form, but since they modify verbs they do not need to make agreement:

Il lit ***plus souvent que*** *son copain.*	He reads **more often than** his friend.
Je cours ***moins vite que*** *vous.*	I run **more slowly than** you.
Elles sortent ***aussi fréquemment que*** *nous.*	They go out **as often as** we do.

The adverbs *bien* and *mal* continue to follow their own rules in the comparative. You may come across the following comparative versions of *bien* and *mal*:

bien		***mal***	
mieux (que)	better (than)	*plus mal que*	worse than
moins bien que	less well than	*moins mal que*	less poorly than
aussi bien que	as well as	*aussi mal que*	as poorly as

Note that, as with the adjective form, *pis* may be seen as a literary form of "worse."

Elle danse **mieux que** *son amie.*	She dances **better than** her friend.
J'écris **moins mal qu'***avant.*	I'm writing **less poorly than** before.
Tu chantes **aussi bien que** *ton mari.*	You sing **as well as** your husband.
Nous jouons **plus mal qu'***eux.*	We play **worse** than they do.

Work with it

A. Which comparison word makes the most sense with the given adverb in the following sentences? Circle your answer, and underline the adverb.

1. Les léopards courent [plus/moins/aussi] vite que les éléphants.
2. On boit le champagne [plus/moins/aussi] souvent que l'eau.
3. Les enfants attendent [plus/moins/aussi] patiemment que les adultes.
4. Les professeurs sortent [plus/moins/aussi] fréquemment que leurs étudiants.
5. Les couturiers s'habillent [plus/moins/aussi] élégamment que les comptables.

B. How would you translate the *bien/mal* comparisons in these sentences?

1. Les animaux sont traités **plus mal que** les humains. ___________
2. Les musiciens jouent **aussi bien que** les acteurs. _____________
3. Je me sens **moins bien qu'**hier. ____________________________
4. Le concert allait **moins bien que** je voulais. ________________
5. Elle cuisine **mieux** quand elle écoute de la musique. ___________

Comparing nouns: When nouns are the focus of a comparative expression, there are a couple of differences. The words "*de* + noun" follow the comparison word, and where the amounts are equal, *autant* is used instead of *aussi*.

J'ai **plus de livres que** *toi.*	I have **more books than** you.
Il a **moins de cheveux que** *son père.*	He has **less hair than** his father.
Nous avons **autant d'argent que** *nos parents.*	We have **as much money as** our parents.

Comparing verbs: Sometimes you'll see a comparison that relates directly to the verb rather than to an adverb or adjective.

Il travaille ***moins que*** *sa soeur.*	He works **less than** his sister.
Nous lisons ***plus que*** *vous.*	We read **more than** you do.
Je mange ***autant que*** *mon ami.*	I eat **as much as** my friend.

Work with it

For the following sentences, determine whether a noun or a verb is being compared.

1. Les acteurs chantent plus que les biologistes. noun/verb

2. Son mari a plus d'amis qu'elle. noun/verb

3. Vous avez plus de chiens que vos voisins. noun/verb

4. Il s'amuse plus que son collègue. noun/verb

5. Elles voyagent plus que leurs pairs. noun/verb

6. Nous avons moins de voitures que vous. noun/verb

Superlative of adjectives: The superlative construction drops the comparative *que* and gains a definite article. You'll notice that the definite article is repeated, once in front of the noun and again in front of the superlative expression.

C'est ***la fille la plus intéressante*** *du groupe.*	She's **the most interesting girl** of the group.
Paul est ***l'étudiant le plus paresseux****.*	Paul is **the laziest student**.
Tu as acheté ***les écouteurs les moins chers****?*	Did you buy **the cheapest headphones**?

Note that in some cases, the larger group is delimited and in other cases it isn't. For instance, in the first sentence it's specified that she is the most interesting girl *of the group*. This could be accomplished in the second sentence as well by adding *de* + some group, e.g. *Paul est l'étudiant le plus paresseux de la classe* (Paul is the laziest student in the class).

The situation is less complicated for *meilleur* and *pire,* which just need an article:

*C'est **le meilleur livre** que j'ai trouvé.*	It's the best book that I've found.
*Lundi c'est **le pire jour** de la semaine.*	Monday is the worst day of the week.

For adjectives that generally come before the noun, you'll see one of two possible constructions in the superlative, as in the following pairs of sentences:

*C'est **le plus jeune garçon**.* *C'est **le garçon le plus jeune**.*	He is **the youngest boy**.
*C'est **la plus belle fille** du monde.* *C'est **la fille la plus belle** du monde.*	She is **the most beautiful girl** in the world.
*C'est **la plus grande maison** du quartier.* *C'est **la maison la plus grande** du quartier.*	It's **the biggest house** in the neighborhood.

Superlative of adverbs: The superlative with adverbs is less complicated. The definite article is always *le,* since adverbs don't have to make gender or number agreement. There's also no repetition of the definite article, since the antecedent is a verb rather than a noun.

*Il court **le plus lentement**.*	He runs **the most slowly**.
*Je mange **le plus vite**.*	I eat **the fastest**.
*Elles sortent **le plus souvent**.*	They go out **the most often**.
*Vous souriez **le plus gentiment**.*	You smile **the most kindly**.

The adverbs *bien* and *mal* continue to follow irregular patterns in the superlative. The superlative of *bien* is *le mieux* and the superlative of *mal* is *le pis* or *le plus mal.*

*De tous nos amis, c'est elle qui chante **le mieux**.*	Of all our friends, she sings **the best**.
*C'est Paul qui fait **le plus mal**.*	It's Paul who is doing **the worst**.

Superlative of nouns: Again, in order to move from comparative to superlative, all that's needed is the addition of the definite article *le*.

C'est moi qui ai ***le plus de livres****.*	I have **the most books**.
C'est lui qui a ***le moins de cheveux****.*	He has **the least hair**.

Superlative of verbs: The same goes for the superlative of verbs: the comparison is removed and the definite article *le* is added.

Il travaille ***le moins****.*	He works **the least**.
Nous lisons ***le plus****.*	We read **the most**.

Work with it

A. In the following sentences, translate the comparison in bold.

1. C'est **le meilleur souvenir** de mon enfance. ____________
2. Il a **les pires idées** de notre classe. ____________
3. Ce sont **les meilleurs amis** du monde. ____________
4. Elle a **le plus mauvais propriétaire** du quartier. ____________

B. Read the following paragraph, identify the eight comparative constructions, and sort them into the table below based on what they compare.

Arthur est un garçon de 8 ans. Parmi les enfants du quartier, il a le plus d'amis parce que c'est lui le plus bavard de tous. Grâce à son abondance d'amis, Arthur sort le plus souvent et il joue le plus. Il est aussi invité le plus fréquemment chez les autres pour dîner parce qu'il est le moins difficile en ce qui concerne la nourriture, et parce qu'il se plaint le moins. C'est pour toutes ses raisons qu'il a le plus de confiance en soi.

Adjectives	Adverbs	Nouns	Verbs

C. Translate the following quote from *Esprit des Lois* by Montesquieu (1892).

Le droit des gens est naturellement fondé sur ce principe, que les diverses nations doivent se faire dans la paix le plus de bien, et dans la guerre le moins de mal qu'il est possible.

____

____

____

____

IV. Reading and translation

Read the following excerpt from *Autour de la Table* by George Sand (1876) and answer the questions below.

Quelle table? C'est chez les Montfeuilly qu'elle se trouve; c'est une grande, une vilaine table. C'est Pierre Bonnin, le menuisier de leur village, qui l'a faite, il y a tantôt vingt ans. Il l'a faite avec un vieux merisier de leur jardin. **Elle est longue, elle est ovale, il y a place pour beaucoup de monde**. Elle a des pieds à mourir de rire; des pieds qui ne pouvaient sortir que du cerveau de Pierre Bonnin, grand inventeur de formes incommodes et inusitées.

Enfin c'est une table qui ne paie pas de mine, mais c'est une solide, une fidèle, une honnête table, elle n'a jamais voulu tourner; **elle ne parle pas, elle n'écrit pas**, elle n'en pense peut-être pas moins, mais elle ne fait pas connaître de quel esprit elle est possédée: **elle cache ses opinions**.

1 How many adjectives are used to describe the table? Are they generally positive or negative?

2 Which noun do the adjectives *incommodes* and *inusitées* modify?

3 Translate the highlighted phrases, and then check your answers in the back of the book.

4 More determiners

I. Funny French!

To start: In the dialogue below, you'll see adjectives and nouns that you should recognize as cognates. The word *votre* is something we'll be looking at in this chapter, and it means "your."

Can you understand the joke on the first try?

Quelle est votre
principale qualité?
Je suis très rapide en
calcul mental.
23 x 543?
37.
C'est faux.
Oui mais c'est rapide.

Verify: Now check the translation in the back of the book and see if you were right. The most important thing is that you get the gist, but also look at the individual words you weren't too sure about and make a mental note of their meaning for future reference.

II. Vocabulary

In this chapter we're going to look at some other possible types of determiners, i.e. words that go in front of nouns. So far we've seen three examples of determiners: definite, indefinite, and partitive articles. These are the most common determiners, but sometimes other types of determiners will either supplement or take the place of articles. Here we'll analyze the case of numbers, demonstrative determiners, and possessive determiners.

A. Cardinal and ordinal numbers

There are a few things to know about numbers that will be important as you read in French. Although larger numbers, including years, will usually appear in digits rather than being spelled out, it will be helpful to know the lower numbers and their patterns, as well as ordinal numbers. Here I'll show you the basic patterns and abbreviations you're likely to encounter.

Cardinal numbers

0	zéro	10	dix	20	vingt	30	trente	50	cinquante
1	un	11	onze	21	vingt et un	31	trente et un	51	cinquante et un
2	deux	12	douze	22	vingt-deux	32	trente-deux	52	cinquante-deux
3	trois	13	treize	23	vingt-trois	33	trente-trois	53	cinquante-trois
4	quatre	14	quatorze	24	vingt-quatre		. . .		. . .
5	cinq	15	quinze	25	vingt-cinq	40	quarante	60	soixante
6	six	16	seize	26	vingt-six	41	quarante et un	61	soixante et un
7	sept	17	dix-sept	27	vingt-sept	42	quarante-deux	62	soixante-deux
8	huit	18	dix-huit	28	vingt-huit	43	quarante-trois	63	soixante-trois
9	neuf	19	dix-neuf	29	vingt-neuf		. . .		. . .

As you can see, French numbers follow a fairly regular pattern up through the sixties. Things get interesting once we hit 70, and this is where some learners start to get confused. Check out the cardinal numbers from 70 through 99.

70	soixante-dix	80	quatre-vingts	90	quatre-vingt-dix
71	soixante et onze	81	quatre-vingt-un	91	quatre-vingt-onze
72	soixante-douze	82	quatre-vingt-deux	92	quatre-vingt-douze
73	soixante-treize	83	quatre-vingt-trois	93	quatre-vingt-treize
74	soixante-quatorze	84	quatre-vingt-quatre	94	quatre-vingt-quatorze
75	soixante-quinze	85	quatre-vingt-cinq	95	quatre-vingt-quinze
76	soixante-seize	86	quatre-vingt-six	96	quatre-vingt-seize
77	soixante-dix-sept	87	quatre-vingt-sept	97	quatre-vingt-dix-sept
78	soixante-dix-huit	88	quatre-vingt-huit	98	quatre-vingt-dix-huit
79	soixante-dix-neuf	89	quatre-vingt-neuf	99	quatre-vingt-dix-neuf

As you can see, once you get beyond 69 the numbers start to combine and you have to do a little bit of math to know which number you're looking at.

Ordinal numbers

Luckily, ordinal numbers (e.g. first, second, third, fourth, etc.) are actually quite simple in French. With the exception of the number one, the letters *-ième* are added to the cardinal number. These are abbreviated with the superscript *-e*.

Whereas the number one has its own ordinal format (*premier* and *première*), subsequent numbers that refer to the number "one," such as "first," "twenty-first," etc., follow the same rules as other numbers.

premier/première	$1^{er}/1^{re}$	first
deuxième	2^{e}	second
troisième	3^{e}	third
quatrième	4^{e}	fourth
. . .		
dixième	10^{e}	tenth
onzième	11^{e}	eleventh
douzième	12^{e}	twelfth
. . .		
vingtième	20^{e}	twentieth
vingt et unième	21^{e}	twenty-first
vingt-deuxième	22^{e}	twenty-second
. . .		
trentième	30^{e}	thirtieth
trente et unième	31^{e}	thirty-first
trente-deuxième	32^{e}	thirty-second
. . .		

Work with it

A. Let's do a quick matching exercise to work on recognizing the written forms of cardinal and ordinal numbers.

1. quarante-trois	**a.** seventy-eighth
2. dixième	**b.** twenty-six
3. quatre-vingt-septième	**c.** thirteen
4. vingt-six	**d.** tenth
5. treize	**e.** eighty-seventh
6. soixante-dix-huitième	**f.** forty-three
7. soixante-quatrième	**g.** sixty-fourth

B. Paying attention to the context, which form of the number would you see in the following sentences? Circle either the cardinal or ordinal form.

1. C'est la [cinq/cinquième] fois qu'elle me téléphone aujourd'hui.
2. Tu as fait la connaissance de ma petite nièce? Elle a [trois/troisième] ans.
3. Il travaille sur ce projet depuis [deux/deuxième] semaines.
4. Ils accueillent un [quatre/quatrième] enfant dans leur famille.
5. Mon mari a trouvé [cent/centième] dollars dans la rue!
6. Elle vient d'écrire son [trente/trentième] roman.
7. Nous avons l'intention de regarder [dix/dixième] films ce weekend.

B. Demonstrative determiners

Demonstrative determiners are so called because they *demonstrate* which noun in particular is being referenced. Whereas definite, indefinite, and partitive articles refer to things in a more general way (e.g. "the girls in the room," or "some cake"), demonstrative determiners refer to specific things or people.

They correspond to the English words "this," "that," "these," or "those." Here is a list of demonstrative determiners in French:

Singular (masc.)	Singular (fem.)	Plural (masc.)	Plural (fem.)
ce (cet)	*cette*	*ces*	*ces*

Just as with articles, demonstrative determiners go in front of a noun, and they agree in gender and number with the noun they modify. *Cet* is used for masculine nouns that start with a vowel.

Je ne connais pas ***ces*** *hommes.*	I do not know **these** men.
Il aime bien ***cette*** *voiture.*	He really likes **this** car.
Tu vois ***ce*** *livre?*	Do you see **this** book?
Nous achetons ***cet*** *ordinateur.*	We are buying **this** computer.

Work with it

Read the following short dialogue and fill in the table that follows with the demonstrative determiners and nouns you can find, along with their corresponding gender. I've done the first one as a model.

A: Bonjour, madame. Puis-je vous aider?

B: Oui, je cherche un cadeau pour une amie. Elle est chimiste et elle adore les chiens.

A: Alors je pourrais vous suggérer ce livre – il est très apprécié par les scientifiques.

B: Hmm . . . elle n'aime pas trop lire dans son temps libre. Vous auriez quelque chose d'autre?

A: Bien sûr! Si elle aime les chiens, nous avons aussi cette figurine en porcelaine.

B: Oui, c'est mignon. . . . Je préfère plutôt ces cartes à jouer, par contre elle n'y joue pas souvent.

A: Qu'est-ce que vous pensez alors de ce coussin décoratif avec des équations?

B: Ah, c'est parfait! Je le prends. Merci, madame.
A: Je vous en prie. Cet objet figure parmi nos meilleures ventes. C'est un très bon choix!

	Demonstrative det.	Noun	Gender
1	*ce*	*livre*	*masculine*
2			
3			
4			
5			

C. Possessive determiners

Like demonstrative determiners, possessive determiners replace the article in front of nouns. Rather than referring to a specific thing or person, possessive determiners indicate to whom they belong. Here is a list of French possessive determiners (in their masculine, feminine, and plural forms) and their English counterparts:

mon/ma/mes	my	*notre/nos*	our
ton/ta/tes	your	*votre/vos*	your
son/sa/ses	his/her	*leur/leurs*	their

Here are some examples of how these work with nouns:

mes chaussures	my shoes	*notre mariage*	our marriage
ton appartement	your apartment	*vos parents*	your parents
sa valise	his/her suitcase	*leur opinion*	their opinion

Pronunciation note: As I've mentioned a couple of times so far, French doesn't like having two vowels next to each other. You've seen examples of elision (e.g. *l'art, l'option*, or *n'est*). You've also seen an example (just above, in demonstrative determiners) where an alternate masculine form ending in a consonant is used instead (*cet* as opposed to the usual *ce*). Neither of these things happens with possessive determiners. Instead, when a feminine noun starts with a vowel, the masculine determiner is used. For example:

mon opinion	my opinion
son attitude	his/her attitude

Work with it

Fill in the list with either the missing possessive determiner in French or noun in English.

mon projet	my project	*ton cours*	your class
_____ *idée*	my idea	____ *compagnie*	your company
mes enfants	my children	*tes collègues*	your colleagues
son travail	his/her job	______ *invité*	our guest
sa chambre	his/her _____	*notre maison*	our _______
______ *clés*	his/her keys	*nos recettes*	our recipes
______ *portable*	your cell phone	*leur amour*	their love
votre imprimante	your printer	______ *passion*	their passion
vos dossiers	your files	*leurs lettres*	their letters

III. Grammar

A. *Cardinal and ordinal numbers*

Both cardinal and ordinal numbers are considered determiners, since they precede the noun and provide a further point of reference. While cardinal numbers (e.g. 1, 2, 3) can sometimes replace an article entirely, they can also be used in conjunction with articles to provide additional information. Consider the difference between the sentences in the first group and those in the second group:

J'ai ***trois*** *chiens.*	I have **three** dogs.
Tu vois ***cinq*** *hommes?*	You see **five** men?
Il veut ***dix*** *tartes.*	He wants **ten** pies.

Les trois *chiens aboient.*	**The three** dogs are barking.
Tu vois ***les cinq*** *hommes?*	You see **the five** men?
Il veut ***les dix*** *tartes.*	He wants **the ten** pies.

In the second group, the addition of a definite article makes it clear that the noun in question (the dogs, the men, the pies) has already been mentioned. Both the speaker and the listener know *which* dogs, *which* men, and *which* pies are being indicated.

Ordinal numbers (e.g. first, second, third) do not have the same flexibility as cardinal numbers. They can only be used along with another determiner, not on their own. They are restricted the same way in English. Consider these sentences:

C'est ***mon troisième*** *jour au travail.*	It's **my third** day at work.
Elle fête ***son dixième*** *anniversaire.*	She's celebrating **her tenth** birthday.
Tu assistes à ***la première*** *réunion ce soir?*	Are you coming to **the first** meeting tonight?
C'est ***la deuxième*** *fois que je le vois.*	It's **the second** time I've seen him.

Notice that in the first two sentences, the ordinal number is used alongside a possessive determiner, while in the last two sentences it's used with a definite article. It can also be used with an indefinite article, as in:

Nous cherchons ***un troisième*** *chat.*	We're looking for **a third** cat.
Ils ont acheté ***une deuxième*** *voiture.*	They bought **a second** car.

Note: There's an interesting difference between French and English with regard to age. Whereas in English we say "I am + number," in French they say "I have + number + years." For instance, "I am 32" would be translated into French as *"J'ai 32 ans."*

Work with it

Now that you can recognize cardinal and ordinal numbers, try your hand at translating these simple sentences.

1. Nous fêtons notre dixième anniversaire de mariage.

   ____

2. Le fils de nos voisins a huit ans, et il veut deux nouveaux ballons de basket.

   ____

3. Tu as regardé le premier discours du président ce soir?

____

4. Nous avons deux chiens, et je désire un troisième.

____

B. *Demonstrative determiners*

As you saw in the Vocabulary section, demonstrative determiners are used to denote specific things or people in the same way we use "this/that/these/those" in English.

Proximity to the speaker is expressed differently in the two languages, however. In English, "this" and "these" refer to things that are close to the speaker while "that" and "those" refer to things that are farther away. In French, the same set of demonstrative determiners can refer to things that are either near or far from the speaker. Proximity can instead be expressed in one of two ways. Either it will be apparent through context, or it can be emphasized with the use of the suffixes *-ci* and *-là*, placed after the noun in question with a hyphen.

*Je veux **ce livre-ci**.*	I want **this book** (here).
*Il m'a donné **cette robe-là**.*	He gave me **that dress** (there).
*Tu cherches **ces gants-ci**?*	Are you looking for **these gloves** (here)?
*Non, je préfère **cette paire-là**.*	No, I prefer **that pair** (there).

Work with it

A. Are the nouns in these sentences masculine or feminine? Singular or plural? Use the demonstrative determiner (and a dictionary, if necessary) to find your answers.

1.	Je n'écoute jamais cette musique.	M/F	S/P
2.	Il m'offre souvent ces compliments.	M/F	S/P
3.	Ce moment est difficile à vivre.	M/F	S/P
4.	Elle comprend bien cet ordinateur.	M/F	S/P
5.	Cette image impressionne tous les élèves.	M/F	S/P

B. In the following sentences, is the object near to the speaker or far away?

1. Tiens, prends ce sac pour ton voyage. Near/Far
2. Cette chemise-ci ne lui plaît pas. Near/Far
3. Ces bottes-là sont parfaites. Near/Far
4. Pourquoi tu manges ce gâteau et pas l'autre? Near/Far
5. Elle n'aime pas trop ce tableau-là. Near/Far

C. *Possessive determiners*

As a reminder, here are the possessive determiners in French.

mon/ma/mes	my	*notre/nos*	our
ton/ta/tes	your	*votre/vos*	your
son/sa/ses	his/her	*leur/leurs*	their

For each subject in the list, you see the masculine form, then the feminine, and finally the plural. You might notice that there are only two choices of possessives for plurals (those that correspond to *nous*, *vous*, and *ils/elles*). This is because there's no distinction for gender. The singular subjects, on the other hand, are differentiated based on gender.

The most important thing to remember about possessive determiners is that the agreement is based on the gender and/or number of the **object** that is possessed, and **not** on the person who possesses it. Let's look at some examples and then break them down.

Il promène ***son*** *chien dans le jardin.*	He's walking his dog in the yard.
Elle promène ***son*** *chien dans le jardin.*	She's walking her dog in the yard.
J'ai perdu ***mon*** *manteau hier.*	I lost my coat yesterday.
J'ai perdu ***ma*** *bague préférée.*	I lost my favorite ring.
Nous allons au cinéma avec ***notre*** *frère.*	We're going to the movies with our brother.
Nous allons au cinéma avec ***notre*** *soeur.*	We're going to the movies with our sister.

Tu vois souvent ***ta*** *famille?*	Do you see your family often?
Tu vois souvent ***ton*** *père?*	Do you see your father often?

Look at the first pair of sentences. Even though the gender of the person changed, the possessive determiner did not: *son* can mean either "his" or "her." It is masculine and singular in this case because the word *chien* is masculine and singular.

The same logic can be applied in the next pair of sentences. It doesn't matter whether *je* refers to a man or a woman, the reason the possessive determiner changes from *mon* to *ma* is because the gender of the object changes from masculine (*manteau*) to feminine (*bague*).

The third pair of sentences illustrates the lack of gender agreement for plural subjects. *Notre* is used regardless of the gender of the thing or person that's possessed.

In the final pair, we see the same situation as in the second set of sentences. *Famille* is feminine and *père* is masculine, hence the change from *ta* to *ton*. The gender of the person behind the *tu* is irrelevant. (Notice also the difference in placement of the adverb compared to English.)

Work with it

A. Read the following sentences and translate the part in bold.

1. Il n'aime pas quand on critique **ses idées**. ____________________
2. Elle voit **son père** chaque samedi. ____________________
3. Nous envoyons des cadeaux à **notre soeur**. ____________________
4. Il oublie toujours de faire **ses devoirs**. ____________________

B. For the following translations, fill in the appropriate French possessive determiner.

1.	I left my coat at the restaurant.	//	J'ai laissé ________ manteau au restaurant.
2.	She doesn't like his attitude.	//	Elle n'aime pas _______ attitude.
3.	We tell our story.	//	Nous racontons _______ histoire.
4.	They're hiding their news.	//	Ils cachent ________ nouvelles.

IV. Reading and translation

Read the following excerpt from *Vie de Jeanne d'Arc* by Anatole France (1908), and answer the questions below.

> **Dans ce petit village de Domremy**, situé à moins de trois lieues en aval de Neufchâteau et à cinq lieues en amont de Vaucouleurs, une fille naquit vers l'an 1410 ou 1412, **destinée à l'existence la plus singulière**. Elle naissait pauvre. Jacques ou Jacquot d'Arc, son père, originaire du village de Ceffonds en Champagne, vivait d'un gagnage ou petite ferme, et menait les chevaux au labour. Ses voisins et voisines le tenaient pour bon chrétien et vaillant à l'ouvrage. Sa femme était originaire de Vouthon, village situé à une lieue et demie au nord-ouest de Domremy, par delà les bois de Greux. Ayant nom Isabelle ou Zabillet, elle reçut, à une époque qu'on ne saurait indiquer, le surnom de Romée. On appelait ainsi ceux qui étaient allés à Rome ou avaient fait quelque grand pèlerinage, et l'on peut croire qu'Isabelle gagna son nom de Romée en prenant les coquilles et le bourdon. **Un de ses frères était curé, un autre, couvreur; un de ses neveux charpentier**. Elle avait déjà donné à son mari trois enfants: Jacques ou Jacquemin, Catherine et Jean.

1 Aside from the years, how many numbers do you see?

2 How many possessive determiners do you see? Can you tell which ones mean "his" (referring to the father) and which ones mean "her" (referring to the mother)?

3 Who are these people in relation to Jeanne d'Arc? How many siblings did she have?

4 Translate the highlighted portions, and check your answers in the back of the book.

The imperfect and the compound past

I. Funny French!

To start: Scan the text for words you know. Can you guess the gist of the joke?

J'ai décidé de commencer mon année 2020 au mois de février.

Je considère que janvier était un mois d'essai gratuit.

Verify: Now look up the words you still don't understand, and translate the joke into English. Check the answer in the back of the book to see how close you were.

II. Vocabulary

A. Verbs

Many French verbs with prefixes will become recognizable to you if you already know their root verb. For example, if you already know the verb *tenir* (to hold), you can probably tell that the following verbs are related to it: *maintenir* (to keep or hold), *obtenir* (to obtain or get), and *retenir* (to catch hold of or retain). Not only are the meanings of these verbs closely related, but they are conjugated the same way as well.

Venir (to come) and its related verbs are conjugated the same way as *tenir* and its related verbs. Here is a list of some of the verbs in this category:

tenir	to hold	*venir*	to come
s'abstenir	to abstain from	*advenir*	to happen
appartenir	to belong to	*contrevenir*	to contravene
contenir	to contain	*convenir*	to suit, be suitable
détenir	to detain	*devenir*	to become
entretenir	to look after, support	*intervenir*	to intervene
maintenir	to maintain, keep, hold	*parvenir*	to reach, achieve
obtenir	to obtain, get	*prévenir*	to warn
retenir	to retain, catch hold of	*revenir*	to come back
soutenir	to support	*se souvenir*	to remember

These verbs are all conjugated following the same pattern:

je tiens	*nous tenons*	Past participle: *tenu*
tu tiens	*vous tenez*	
il/elle/on tient	*ils/elles tiennent*	
je viens	*nous venons*	Past participle: *venu*
tu viens	*vous venez*	
il/elle/on vient	*ils/elles viennent*	

Pronunciation note: All conjugations in the singular (*je, tu, il/elle/on*) sound the same in this pattern, even though they have different endings.

Work with it

In the following sentences, underline the verb that is related to *tenir* and *venir*. Make sure to identify its corresponding subject pronoun and notice how it correlates with the verb ending.

1. Ce sont nos amis; ils viennent souvent chez nous.
2. J'arrive bientôt – est-ce que cela vous convient?
3. Je maintiens toujours une vision positive.
4. Son ami appartient à notre équipe de football.
5. Mes parents deviennent vraiment insupportables.
6. Nous obtenons le résultat voulu.

B. Adverbs of time

As you learn to read in the past tense in French, it will be helpful to memorize some adverbs of time that can serve as added hints to when something happened. Here are some common examples:

actuellement[1]	currently	*après*	after
aujourd'hui	today	*auparavant*	previously, beforehand
avant	before	*bientôt*	soon
d'abord	first	*déjà*	already
enfin	finally	*ensuite*	next
hier	yesterday	*maintenant*	now
récemment	recently	*souvent*	often
tout à coup	suddenly	*toujours*	always

Work with it

In the following sentences, circle the time expression that makes the most sense in context.

1. (Actuellement/Hier) je fais mes devoirs.
2. Il va (souvent/déjà) à la bibliothèque.
3. J'ai fait le ménage (après/avant) la fête.
4. Nous avons (toujours/enfin) reçu nos diplômes.
5. (D'abord/Finalement), vous devez acheter les ingrédients.
6. Elles sont chez le médecin (tout à coup/maintenant).

III. Grammar

A. *The imperfect*

Use: The imperfect is used to express events in the past that were habitual or continuous, or that don't have a distinct starting and stopping point. For example, states of being (to be, to seem, to become) are most frequently expressed using the imperfect since they cannot be defined temporally. The imperfect often corresponds to the English construction "was (verb) ing" or "used to (verb)," but you will see as you read more in French that you can often translate the French imperfect with the English simple past ("(verb)ed").

Formation: The imperfect is formed by taking the present tense *nous* form of the verb, dropping the *-ons,* and adding the appropriate ending for each subject. These endings are:

je	*-ais*	*nous*	*-ions*
tu	*-ais*	*vous*	*-iez*
il/elle/on	*-ait*	*ils/elles*	*-aient*

Using *parler* as an example, we get the stem for the *imparfait* by following the process mentioned above. Then we add the respective endings:

Stem: *parler* → *nous parlons* → *parl-*

je parlais	I was speaking	*nous parlions*	we were speaking
tu parlais	you were speaking	*vous parliez*	you were speaking
il/elle/on parlait	he/she/one was speaking	*ils/elles parlaient*	they were speaking

This conjugation works the same way for *-ir* and *-re* verbs:

Stem: *finir* → *nous finissons* → *finiss-*

je finissais	I was finishing	*nous finissions*	we were finishing
tu finissais	you were finishing	*vous finissiez*	you were finishing
il/elle/on finissait	he/she/one was finishing	*ils/elles finissaient*	they were finishing

Stem: *prendre* → *nous prenons* → *pren-*

je prenais	I was taking	*nous prenions*	we were taking
tu prenais	you were taking	*vous preniez*	you were taking
il/elle/on prenait	he/she/one was taking	*ils/elles prenaient*	they were taking

Note: There is one important exception to this formation rule, and that is the very common verb *être* (to be). Since *être* does not have an *-ons* form in the present tense (*nous sommes*), *ét-* is used as its stem, with the same endings as all the other verbs. For example:

Il était très triste hier.	He was very sad yesterday.
Nous étions toujours à la plage.	We were always at the beach.

Negation: Making a verb negative in the imperfect is easy! It follows the same procedure that's used for the present tense, with *ne* in front of the verb and *pas* after it.

*Je **ne** parlais **pas**.*	I wasn't talking.
*Nous **ne** prenions **pas** le bus.*	We weren't taking the bus.

Work with it

A. In this exercise, translate (out loud) the expression(s) in parentheses into English based on the context of the sentence. Be on the lookout for adverbs or time expressions that help you decide whether to use *"was (verb)ing," "used to (verb),"* or *"(verb)ed."*

1. Quand (j'étais) jeune, (j'aimais) jouer dehors. ________________
2. (Il parlait) au téléphone et (sa mère dessinait). ________________
3. (Nous sortions) toujours pendant nos études universitaires. ____________
4. Hier, (je cuisinais) constamment. ____________________
5. (Vous étiez) mal à l'aise pendant le film? ________________
6. (Les étudiants voulaient) toujours bavarder. ________________

What do you notice? Did you always use the English imperfect? Were you sometimes unsure because two different forms sounded right in context?

B. Now, look back at the verbs in exercise A. Next to each sentence, write out the infinitive (unconjugated) form of all the verbs.

B. *The compound past* (le passé composé)

Use: Contrary to the imperfect, the compound past in French is used to talk about actions that were both started and completed in the past and that were not habitual. You should be able to identify clear time boundaries for these actions. For example, "He bought a car" or "She went to the store" – once the car was purchased or she arrived at the store, the action was done. The compound past in French is usually translated as the simple past in English (or sometimes as the perfect, such as "I have gone" or "He has finished").

Formation: As its name indicates, the compound past is formed using two words (rather than one word with a stem and ending, as in the imperfect). These two words are the auxiliary verb and the past participle. Most verbs use the word *avoir* as their auxiliary, but some use the verb *être*.

To recognize the compound past of a verb, you need to know how *avoir* and *être* are conjugated in the present tense and you need to know the past participle of the main verb being used.

*Il **a mangé** une crêpe.*	He ate a crêpe.
*Nous **avons vu** un oiseau.*	We saw a bird.
*J'**ai chanté**.*	I sang.
*Elles **ont pleuré**.*	They cried.
*Elle **est allée** au marché.*	She went to the market.
*Vous **êtes tombés**.*	You fell.

To recognize past participles, you can rely to some extent on the following rules:

- the past participle of most -*er* verbs will end in -*é*
- the past participle of most -*ir* verbs will end in -*i*
- the past participle of most -*re* verbs will end in -*u*

Examples: *parlé, donné, allé, fini, parti, sorti, rendu, tenu, venu*

Be careful, however, because there are always exceptions to these rules! This is especially true for some irregular but very common verbs, like *être, faire,* and *avoir,* whose past participles are *été, fait,* and *eu.* In addition, some verbs have very short past participles. For example, the past participles for *savoir, lire, devoir,* and *pouvoir* are *su, lu, dû,* and *pu,* respectively.

Note: You may have noticed that for verbs taking *être* as their auxiliary, the past participle agrees in gender and number with the subject. This is why "*Elle est allée*" has an extra 'e' for feminine and "*Vous êtes tombés*" has an "s" for plural. Verbs that take *avoir* as their auxiliary do not make agreement.

Negation: Negation in the compound past is slightly different since two verbs are involved instead of just one. In this case, the *ne . . . pas* goes around the auxiliary verb, not the past participle.

*Il **n'**a **pas** chanté.*	He did not sing.
*Nous **ne** sommes **pas** sortis.*	We did not go out.

Work with it

A. In the sentences below, identify the auxiliary verb and the past participle, using the infinitive form of each, and following the format in the example below.

Sentence	Auxiliary verb	Past participle
Ex: Je suis allée au marché hier.	suis/être	allée/aller
Il a vu des poissons.	______	______
Tu as acheté des pommes?	______	______
Elles sont venues chez moi.	______	______
Vous avez eu un accident?	______	______
Je suis tombé de ma chaise.	______	______
Elle est née le 19 janvier.	______	______

B. Do you remember how to negate sentences in the imperfect and the compound past? Rewrite the sentences below, adding *ne . . . pas* to make them negative.

1. Elle est allée à la bibliothèque. ______
2. Nous étions mal à l'aise. ______
3. Vous avez dit la même chose. ______
4. Tu jouais dehors. ______
5. Je suis sortie avec elle. ______

C. Translate the following short sentences into English.

1. Nous avons fini le projet. ______.
2. Il est allé chez son voisin. ______.
3. Vous êtes sortis hier soir? ______.
4. Elle a pris le petit déjeuner. ______.

C. Narration

Narrating the past in French involves a combination of the imperfect and the compound past. The imperfect is used to set the scene by describing actions and physical details in the background ("The birds *were chirping*," "It *was* a beautiful day," etc.), and to describe actions that were taking place when something else interrupted them ("I *was working* when he called"). The compound past is then used to describe the intervening actions or anything that was completed in the past.

Work with it

To start: Scan the following short text, underlining examples of the imperfect and circling examples of the compound past. Then, read through it more carefully and try to actively understand why the imperfect or the compound past was used in each case.

> C'était un beau jour d'été. Le soleil brillait, les gens souriaient, et je me sentais tranquille. Je me promenais dans le parc quand tout à coup j'ai vu mon ami Marc. Il marchait vers son bureau mais dès qu'il m'a aperçu, il s'est arrêté pour bavarder un peu. Nous discutions de nos familles quand il a commencé à pleuvoir. Nous avons continué à parler pendant quelques moments et puis j'ai dû retourner au travail. Alors on s'est dit "Au revoir."

Verify: Were there any time-related words or expressions that gave you hints about when the compound past would be used?

IV. Reading and translation

Read the following excerpt from *Clair de lune* by Guy de Maupassant (1884), paying close attention to the use of the imperfect and the compound past, then answer the post-reading questions.

> Il portait bien son nom de bataille, l'abbé Marignan. C'était un grand prêtre maigre, fanatique, d'âme toujours exaltée, mais droite. Toutes ses croyances étaient fixes, sans jamais d'oscillations. **Il s'imaginait sincèrement connaître son Dieu, pénétrer ses desseins, ses volontés, ses intentions**.

Quand il se promenait à grands pas dans l'allée de son petit presbytère de campagne, quelquefois une interrogation se dressait dans son esprit: "Pourquoi Dieu a-t-il fait cela?" Et il cherchait obstinément, prenant en sa pensée la place de Dieu, et il trouvait presque toujours. . . .

Tout lui paraissait créé dans la nature avec une logique absolue et admirable. Les "Pourquoi" et les "Parce que" se balançaient toujours. Les aurores étaient faites pour rendre joyeux les réveils, les jours pour mûrir les moissons, les pluies pour les arroser, les soirs pour préparer au sommeil et les nuits sombres pour dormir.

1 Who is the person being described? What is his profession?

2 Why are the vast majority of the verbs in the imperfect?

3 Find the one verb that is in the *passé composé*. How is it different from the rest?

4 Translate the two highlighted sentences, and check your answers in the back of the book.

____

____

____

____

Note

1 Notice that *actuellement* is a false friend. Rather than "actually," it means "currently." You may remember this from the preliminary chapter, in the section on *faux amis*.

6 Reflexive and reciprocal verbs

I. Funny French!

To start: The word *bonheur* means "happiness." Knowing this, use context clues to try to guess the meaning of unknown words.

Les 4 secrets du bonheur:
- Se réveiller
- Désactiver l'alarme
- Se tourner de l'autre côté
- Se rendormir

Verify: Are there any words you still don't understand? Look them up, and translate the joke out loud. Check your answer in the back of the book.

II. Vocabulary

A. Common reflexive verbs

Reflexive verbs don't look the same in French as they do in English. Instead of adding a version of "self" after the verb (myself, himself, ourselves, etc.), a reflexive pronoun is placed in front of the verb. When you see a reflexive verb in its infinitive, or unconjugated, form (for instance, if you look it up in the dictionary), it will have the third person pronoun *se* in front of it.

Here are some of the most common French reflexive verbs:

s'asseoir	to sit down	*se brosser*	to brush
se casser	to break	*se coucher*	to go to bed
se dépêcher	to hurry	*se déshabiller*	to get undressed
s'énerver	to get annoyed	*se fâcher*	to get angry
s'habiller	to get dressed	*s'habituer à*	to get used to
se laver	to wash	*se lever*	to get up
se raser	to shave	*se reposer*	to relax
se réveiller	to wake up	*se souvenir de*	to remember

Work with it

Complete each sentence with the reflexive verb from the list above that makes the most sense. Remember to look for words you know and pay attention to context clues. ***Note***: The verb will be in the infinitive form here; you'll learn how they're conjugated in the next section.

1. Puisque je suis toujours en retard, ma mère me dit souvent qu'il faut ____________.

2. Elles détestent ____________________ les jambes donc elles portent toujours un jean.

3. Mon ami Paul n'aime pas sortir tous les soirs; il préfère ______________ chez lui.

4. J'ai tendance à ____________________ tôt, mais je reste au lit pendant 20 minutes.

5. Si on veut maigrir, il faut ____________________ faire de l'exercice.

B. *Common reciprocal verbs*

Reciprocal verbs in French differ from their English counterparts as well. This time, a reflexive pronoun is placed in front of the verb instead of adding "each other" after it.

Here are some of the most common French reciprocal verbs:

s'aimer	to love each other	*se comprendre*	to understand each other
se disputer	to argue	*s'embrasser*	to kiss each other
s'entendre	to get along	*se parler*	to talk to each other
se quitter	to leave each other	*se rencontrer*	to meet each other
se téléphoner	to call each other	*se voir*	to see each other

Work with it

A. Look at the pictures below and decide which reciprocal verb from the list above best describes what is happening. Don't worry about conjugation – just write the infinitive, and don't forget the reflexive pronoun.

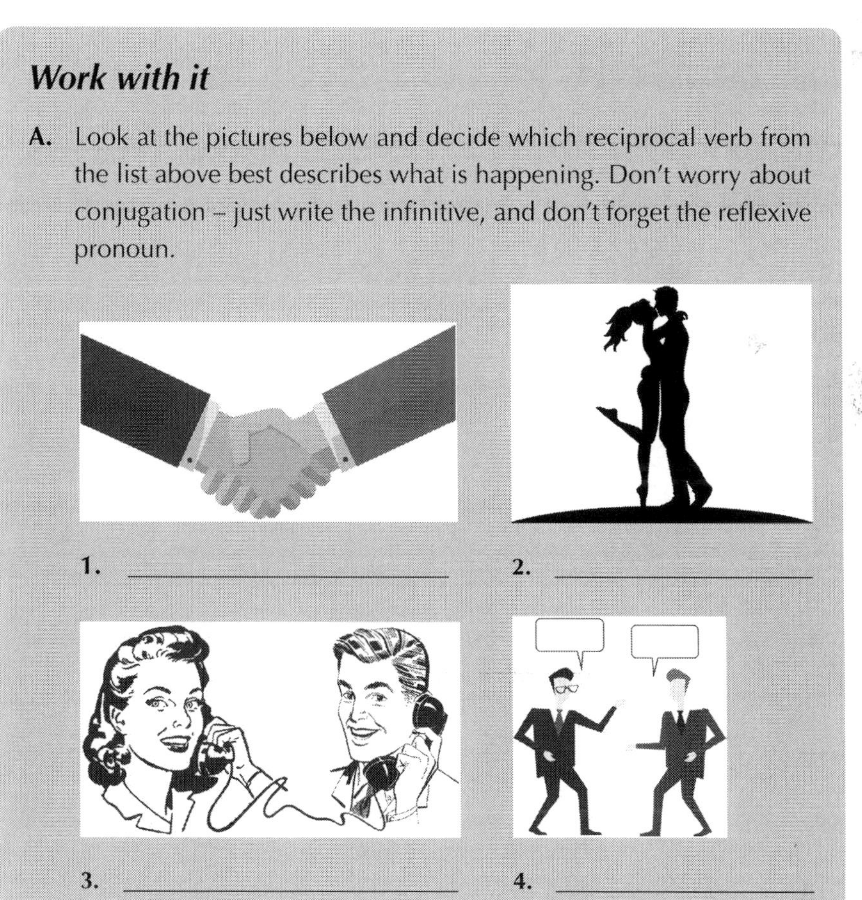

1. ______________________ **2.** ______________________

3. ______________________ **4.** ______________________

B. Read the following sentences. Based on what is described, which reciprocal verb makes the most sense? Carefully read each sentence and decide which verb best fits the situation, then write that verb on the line.

1. Une femme et son mari ne sont pas d'accord. ______________
2. Deux amis tiennent une conversation. ______________
3. Un étudiant voit son prof pour la première fois. ______________
4. Mes parents sont toujours contents ensemble. ______________
5. Un couple décide de divorcer. ______________

C. Body parts

Knowing the words for certain body parts can come in handy when reading French reflexive verbs.

le bras	arm	*les cheveux*	hair
les dents	teeth	*la jambe*	leg
les mains	hands	*le nez*	nose
le pied	foot	*le visage*	face

You will notice that when body parts are included in a reflexive sentence, French does not use a possessive adjective (my, his, your, etc.). The reflexive pronoun already indicates that the action is being done to oneself, so the adjective would be redundant. Look at the following examples with their English translations:

Elle se rase ***les*** *jambes.*	She shaves **her** legs.
Il se brosse ***les*** *dents.*	He brushes **his** teeth.
Nous nous lavons ***les*** *mains.*	We wash **our** hands.
Je me casse ***le*** *bras.*	I break **my** arm.

Work with it

Circle the body part that makes the most sense in the context of the sentence.

1. Mon petit cousin s'est cassé (le nez/la jambe) en attrapant le ballon de football.
2. Il faut toujours se laver (les cheveux/les mains) avant de manger.
3. Je me lave (le visage/les pieds) avant d'aller voir la pédicure.
4. Elle est trop vaniteuse; elle se brosse (les cheveux/les dents) trois fois par jour.
5. Vous allez vous casser (la jambe/les dents) si vous continuez à sauter en parachute!

III. Grammar

A. Reflexive pronouns

Both reflexive and reciprocal verbs are considered *pronominal*, because they use pronouns. The difference between the two groups is that reflexive actions are done *to oneself*, while reciprocal actions are done *to each other*. The pronouns are the same for both groups of verbs, though, and are referred to collectively as reflexive pronouns. The only thing that differs between the two types of verbs is your understanding of who is performing the action and to/for/on whom.

Let's look at the reflexive pronouns with their respective subject pronouns:

je	*me*	*nous*	*nous*
tu	*te*	*vous*	*vous*
il/elle/on	*se*	*ils/elles*	*se*

Use: In reflexive verbs, the implication is that the action is done both by and to the same person. Sometimes verbs that are not reflexive in English are reflexive in French and vice versa, so keep that in mind while you read or translate.

Here are some examples, with the reflexive pronoun highlighted. Notice that none of them would be translated as reflexive in English.

Je ***me*** *lève tôt.*	I get up early.
Nous ***nous*** *habillons vite.*	We get dressed quickly.
Il ***s'****est cassé le bras.*	He broke his arm.
Tu ***te*** *couches tard.*	You go to bed late.
*Asseyez-****vous****.*	Sit down.
Elles ***se*** *brossent les dents.*	They brush their teeth.

In reciprocal verbs, the implication is that the action is done by one person to another, and vice versa. Since reciprocal verbs necessarily involve two or more people, you will see them used with plural subject pronouns (i.e. *nous, vous, ils,* or *elles*). An exception to this rule is the subject pronoun *on,* which is commonly used in place of *nous* in spoken French.

Ils ***se*** *voient.*	They see each other.
Nous ***nous*** *aimons.*	We love each other.
Vous ***vous*** *écrivez.*	You write to each other.
Ils ***se*** *serrent la main.*	They shake hands.
Elles ***s'****embrassent.*	They kiss (each other).
Nous ***nous*** *parlons.*	We talk to each other.

Pronunciation note: Reflexive pronouns can undergo elision when followed by a word that starts with a vowel. You see an example of this above in the verb *s'embrasser.* It also happens with the reflexive pronouns *me* and *te.*

Work with it

A. In the following sentences, identify the pronominal verb and its pronoun. Using contextual clues, decide whether the verb is reflexive or reciprocal and whether it is past or present tense.

1.	Il se regarde souvent dans le miroir.	reflexive/reciprocal	past/present
2.	Ses parents ne s'entendent pas bien.	reflexive/reciprocal	past/present
3.	Nous nous sommes promenés au parc.	reflexive/reciprocal	past/present
4.	Tu te fâches très facilement!	reflexive/reciprocal	past/present
5.	Ils se sont embrassés fort.	reflexive/reciprocal	past/present

B. Given the reflexive pronoun in each of the following sentences, fill in the appropriate subject pronoun (*je, tu, il/elle/on, nous, vous*, or *ils/elles*). You can follow the example below:

Ex: Il se lève à 9h00 du matin.

1. ____________________ nous promenons souvent au parc.

2. ____________________ te rases tous les jours?

3. ____________________ vous brossez les dents avant de manger?

4. ____________________ se réveille souvent avant moi.

5. ____________________ me souviens de ce jour-là.

6. ____________________ se reposent en faisant du yoga.

C. Now take a moment to think through the translation of each of the sentences in exercise B. Notice whether or not you would use a reflexive construction in English, and make a mental note that these actions are reflexive in French.

B. Conjugation of pronominal verbs

Present tense: You've probably noticed that aside from adding the reflexive pronoun between the subject and verb, nothing changes in the present tense. The verb is still conjugated based on its subject and according to the rules of its group (*-er, -ir, -re,* or irregular). The pronoun is placed between the subject and the verb.

*Il **se** lave les cheveux.*	He washes/is washing his hair.
*Je **me** promène.*	I walk/am walking.
*Vous **vous** aimez.*	You love each other.

Past tense: Recall that the past tense has two possible configurations: the imperfect and the compound past. As before, the imperfect is the easier of the two constructions, since the reflexive pronoun will still be placed between the subject and verb, as it is in the present tense:

Il ***se*** *lavait les cheveux.*	He was washing his hair.
Je ***me*** *promenais.*	I was walking.
Vous ***vous*** *aimiez.*	You loved each other/used to love each other.

The compound past is more difficult, since it has the additional auxiliary verb to consider. In this case, the reflexive pronoun stays out in front of the auxiliary verb.

Il ***s'****est lavé les cheveux.*	He washed his hair.
Je ***me*** *suis promené.*	I walked.
Vous ***vous*** *êtes aimés.*	You loved each other.

Negation: Look at the three constructions below and note the position of the *ne . . . pas*. Do you see the difference between the compound past and the other types?

Present	Imperfect	Compound past
Il ***ne*** *se lave* ***pas*** *les cheveux.*	*Il* ***ne*** *se lavait* ***pas*** *les cheveux.*	*Il* ***ne*** *s'est* ***pas*** *lavé les cheveux.*
Je ***ne*** *me promène* ***pas****.*	*Je* ***ne*** *me promenais* ***pas****.*	*Je* ***ne*** *me suis* ***pas*** *promené.*
Vous ***ne*** *vous aimez* ***pas****.*	*Vous* ***ne*** *vous aimiez* ***pas****.*	*Vous* ***ne*** *vous êtes* ***pas*** *aimés.*

Work with it

A. Present or past? Read each sentence carefully, paying attention to the clues telling you when something happened (e.g. other verb tenses, adverbs of time, etc.). Circle the form of the verb that best fits the sentence.

1. Quand j'étais étudiante, je (me lève/me levais) tôt pour étudier à la bibliothèque.

2. Maintenant, mes amis (se retrouvent/se retrouvaient) pour étudier ensemble au café.
3. D'habitude, nous (nous voyons/nous voyions) trois fois par semaine.
4. Auparavant, ma meilleure amie (se repose/se reposait) au lieu d'étudier.
5. Récemment, elle a changé d'avis et on (se soutient/se soutenait) mutuellement.

B. Do you remember the distinction between imperfect and compound past? In this exercise, match the French sentence fragments on the left with their English equivalent on the right.

1. Elle s'habillait . . .	**a.** I woke up
2. Nous nous sommes vus . . .	**b.** You used to love each other
3. Je me suis réveillé . . .	**c.** We saw each other
4. Tu te dépêchais . . .	**d.** She was getting dressed
5. Vous vous aimiez . . .	**e.** They left each other
6. Ils se sont quittés . . .	**f.** You were hurrying

C. Now, using the reading strategies and the words you've learned so far, decide which of the following best completes the unfinished sentences above by putting the number of that sentence in the corresponding blank below.

_________ . . . parce qu'il était tard.

_________ . . . au restaurant.

_________ . . . quand vous étiez jeunes.

_________ . . . quand il est arrivé.

_________ . . . parce qu'ils ne s'aimaient plus.

_________ . . . à 11h00 ce matin.

D. Translate the following sentences into English, paying attention to the tense. Keep in mind that although French uses a reflexive pronoun, sometimes in English the reflexive or reciprocal nature of the action is implied.

1. Je me lavais les cheveux quand le téléphone a sonné.

____

2. Tu te réveilles chaque jour avant ton fils?

____

3. Elle courait dans le parc quand elle s'est cassé le pied.

____

C. *Reflexive verbs and the passive voice*

The passive voice is used to indicate that the subject is being acted upon, rather than doing the action. In English this is achieved by using the format "is/was + verbed + by." For example, "He was hit by the car" (rather than "The car hit him") or "The book was read by many people" (rather than "Many people read the book").

This construction can be accomplished in French the same way: using *être* (in the present, past, or future tense), the past participle, and one of two possible prepositions: *par* or *de*. If the verb expresses an action, *par* is used. If the verb expresses a state of being, *de* is used.

Le chanteur est admiré **de** *ses fans.*	The singer is admired by his fans.
Ce chercheur est respecté **de** *tout le monde.*	This researcher is respected by everybody.
Le gâteau a été mangé **par** *ma soeur.*	The cake was eaten by my sister.
Le film a été fait **par** *mon réalisateur préféré.*	The film was made by my favorite director.

While you will see the passive voice used sometimes in French, it is also incredibly common to see reflexive verbs used in order to avoid the passive construction. These are called passive reflexives, and they are used when there is no agent involved (i.e. no one doing the action to the subject). Some common examples include:

s'appeler	to be called	*s'intéresser à*	to be interested in
se limiter	to be limited to	*se trouver*	to be found (i.e. located)

Any verb can be transformed in this way to avoid the passive construction. Here are some examples of passive reflexives with their more traditional passive counterparts:

Passive reflexive	Passive voice	English translation
Le pain ***se vend*** *ici.*	*Le pain* ***est vendu*** *ici.*	Bread is sold here.
Cela ***se fait*** *souvent.*	*Cela* ***est fait*** *souvent.*	That happens often.
Ce mot ***s'écrit*** *comment?*	*Ce mot* ***est écrit*** *comment?*	How is this word spelled (written)?
Cela ne ***se dit*** *pas.*	*Cela n'****est*** *pas* ***dit****.*	That isn't said.
La maison ***se voit*** *de loin.*	*La maison peut* ***être vue*** *de loin.*	The house can be seen from far away.

Work with it

The following sentences use a reflexive verb to avoid the passive voice. Think about what they mean, and decide how they would best be translated into English.

1. Le français se parle ici. ______________________
2. Il s'intéresse aux maths. ______________________
3. Ce livre se lit souvent. ______________________
4. La glace se mange en été. ______________________
5. Notre journal se vend bien. ______________________
6. Le vin blanc se boit froid. ______________________
7. Ce mot s'écrit comment? ______________________

IV. Reading and translation

Read the following excerpt from *L'ancien régime et la révolution* by Alexis de Tocqueville (1856). Using contextual clues and what you've learned so far, try to understand the gist of the passage, then answer the post-reading questions.

> Quant à eux, **ils savent bien que la révolution française est un accident local et passager** dont il s'agit seulement de tirer parti. Dans

cette pensée, ils conçoivent des desseins, font des préparatifs, contractent des alliances secrètes; ils se disputent entre eux à la vue de cette proie prochaine, se divisent, se rapprochent; il n'y a presque rien à quoi ils ne se préparent, sinon à ce qui va arriver.

Les Anglais, auxquels le souvenir de leur propre histoire et la longue pratique de la liberté politique donnent plus de lumière et d'expérience, **aperçoivent bien comme à travers un voile épais l'image d'une grande Révolution qui s'avance**; mais ils ne peuvent distinguer sa forme, et l'action qu'elle va exercer bientôt sur les destinées du monde et sur la leur propre leur est cachée.

1 Think about the function of the verbs with a reflexive pronoun. Are they reflexive? Reciprocal? Being used to avoid the passive voice?

2 Based on the vocabulary used, what's the main topic? Which words give this impression?

3 Translate the two highlighted phrases, and check your answers in the back of the book.

____

____

____

____

7 Direct and indirect object pronouns

I. Funny French!

To start: In this joke, you should be able to identify several of the words and their functions: the subject pronoun and verb, the adverb *comment,* the noun *café,* the adjective *silencieux*. What do you think the joke says?

TU L'AIMES COMMENT
TON CAFÉ LE MATIN?

Silencieux.

Verify: Check the translation in the back of the book. Now look back at the first couple words of the joke: the *l'* is not translated in the English version. That's because it's acting as a direct object pronoun that corresponds to the words *ton café*, a repetition that doesn't generally happen in English (we wouldn't say "How do you like **it** your coffee in the morning?"). We'll look more at direct and indirect object pronouns in this chapter.

II. Vocabulary

In Chapter 2 we looked at subject pronouns. As a reminder, a pronoun is a word that replaces a noun (whether common or proper). Thus with subject pronouns, we use the words "he/she/they" in order to avoid repeating "Paul" or "The girl" or "My friends" over and over as the subject.

A. Direct object pronouns

The direct object, which is the recipient of the action, is frequently referred to as a COD in French (*complément d'object direct*, or direct object complement).

*J'ouvre **la porte**.*	I open **the door**.
*Il apporte **le pain**.*	He's bringing **the bread**.
*Elle voit souvent **sa mère**.*	She sees **her mother** often.
*Nous préférons **l'art moderne**.*	We prefer **modern art**.
*Tu aimes **ton frère**?*	Do you like **your brother**?
*Elles achètent **les chaussures**.*	They are buying **the shoes**.

The direct object answers the question "*verb* what?" or "*verb* whom?" In the first sentence, the answer to the question "open what?" is "the door." For the third sentence, the answer to "see whom?" is "her mother."

To replace nouns in this position, you will see the following French direct object pronouns:

me (m')	me	*nous*	us
te (t')	you	*vous*	you
le (l')	him/it	*les*	them
la (l')	her/it		

Now consider the same sample sentences from above, with the nouns replaced by direct object pronouns:

Je ***l'****ouvre.*	I open **it**.
Il ***l'****apporte.*	He's bringing **it**.
Elle ***la*** *voit souvent.*	She sees **her** often.
Nous ***le*** *préférons.*	We prefer **it**.
Tu ***l'****aimes?*	Do you like **him**?
Elles ***les*** *achètent.*	They are buying **them**.

The pronouns *me, te, nous,* and *vous* refer only to people, and not to things.

Il ***m'****aime de tout son coeur.*	He loves **me** with all his heart.
Je ***te*** *connais bien.*	I know **you** well.
Vous ***nous*** *suivez?*	Are you following **us**?
Elles ***vous*** *aident.*	They are helping **you**.

Work with it

A. In the following sentences in French, identify and circle the direct object pronoun. Then write out its English counterpart.

1. Il m'aide quand je ne comprends pas. ______________________
2. Tu l'as acheté quand même? ______________________
3. Elle les aime tant. ______________________
4. Je la connais mieux qu'avant. ______________________

B. Now read these sentences in French and identify both the direct object pronoun and the noun it replaces (including its determiner).

Ex: Elle ne s'entend pas bien avec sa soeur donc elle ne la voit pas souvent.

1. Est-ce que tu as vu le film hier soir? Je l'ai détesté.
2. Les chiens sont plus loyaux que les chats; c'est pourquoi on les préfère.
3. L'ordinateur ne fonctionne plus donc je le jette.
4. Il n'a pas répondu à ta question parce qu'il ne l'a pas entendue.

B. Indirect object pronouns

Indirect objects (*complément d'objet indirect,* or COI in French) are the people "to whom" or "for whom" the action happens. They are usually indicated by prepositional phrases, and are seen both in combination with direct objects and on their own.

Je donne un cadeau ***à ma mère***.	I give a gift **to my mother**.
Nous parlons souvent ***à nos amis***.	We often speak **to our friends**.
Il parle ***à moi et ma soeur***.	He speaks **to me and my sister**.
Il fait des biscuits ***pour les enfants***.	He makes cookies **for the children**.

Indirect objects can be replaced by the following pronouns in French:

me (m')	me	*nous*	us
te (t')	you	*vous*	you
lui	him/her	*leur*	them

These sentences would look like this with an indirect object pronoun:

Je ***lui*** *donne un cadeau.*	I give **her** a gift.
Nous ***leur*** *parlons souvent.*	We speak **to them** often.
Il ***nous*** *parle.*	He speaks **to us**.
Il ***leur*** *fait des biscuits.*	He makes **them** cookies.

Note: Some verbs that use prepositions in English do not do so in French and vice versa, meaning a direct object in one language does not necessarily correspond to a direct object in the other language. The same is true for indirect objects. For example, the French verb is *téléphoner à* + someone, necessitating an indirect object pronoun (*Je lui téléphone*), whereas this is not the case in the English sentence "I call her" (direct object pronoun). The reverse is true for the verb *écouter,* which uses a direct object in French (*J'écoute ma mère/Je l'écoute)* and an indirect object in English (I listen to my mother/I listen to her).

Work with it

Identify and underline the indirect object pronoun in the following French sentences. Then write out its English counterpart.

Ex: Ils <u>vous</u> écrivent souvent. <u>you/to you</u>

1. Je leur téléphone chaque nuit. ____________________
2. Il te donne des fleurs. ____________________
3. Elle leur achète une maison. ____________________
4. Tu me parles de tes problèmes. ____________________
5. Vous lui donnez des conseils? ____________________

III. Grammar

A. *Placement of object pronouns*

You may have noticed in the examples above that both direct and indirect object pronouns are placed differently within the sentence in French. Whereas they are found after the verb in English, they precede the verb in French. Look back at a few of the previous examples to consider the difference:

*Il **l'**apporte.*	He's bringing **it**.
*Elle **la** voit souvent.*	She sees **her** often.
*Je **te** connais bien.*	I know **you** well.
*Vous **nous** suivez?*	Are you following **us**?
*Je **lui** donne un cadeau.*	I give **her** a gift.
*Nous **leur** parlons souvent.*	We speak **to them** often.
*Il **nous** parle.*	He speaks **to us**.

These examples are all in the present tense. Let's also look at where object pronouns are placed in other constructions. I mentioned above that object pronouns in French go in front of the verb. To be more specific, in most instances they go in front of a *conjugated* verb. In the *passé composé,* this means that the object pronoun will be found in front of the auxiliary verb.

*Je **l'**ai vue hier.*	I saw **her** yesterday.
*Nous **l'**avons fait la semaine dernière.*	We did **it** last week.
*Vous **les** avez achetés?*	Did you buy **them**?
*Il **leur** a parlé avant de venir.*	He talked **to them** before coming.
*Elles **lui** ont téléphoné l'autre jour.*	They called **him** the other day.

You'll notice that when direct object pronouns precede the verb, as they do above, the past participle agrees in gender and number with the implied direct object. Since the *l'* in the first sentence is referring to "her," the past participle *vu* is spelled *vue*. Likewise, in the third sentence, since the direct object is plural, an *-s-* is added.

The thing that makes this difficult for some learners is that agreement is only made when the direct object *pronoun* is used, since it precedes the verb, and *not* when the object itself is used, since it follows the verb. Consider the following sentence pairs to see the difference:

*J'ai vu **ta soeur** hier.*	I saw your sister yesterday.
*Je **l'**ai vue hier.*	I saw her yesterday.
*Vous avez acheté **les légumes**?*	Did you buy the vegetables?
*Vous **les** avez achetés?*	Did you buy them?

It's for this reason that, as you learn verbs, you should get used to seeing their past participles in various states of agreement. That way you'll know which verb you're seeing and whether it involves a direct object pronoun. You may see the following versions of past participles:

	Masc. singular	**Fem. singular**	**Masc. plural**	**Fem. plural**
donner	*donné*	*donnée*	*donnés*	*données*
vendre	*vendu*	*vendue*	*vendus*	*vendues*
choisir	*choisi*	*choisie*	*choisis*	*choisies*

Negation: When it comes to negating the verb in a sentence with object pronouns, you'll notice that the object pronouns tend to stick to the verb – that is, the *ne . . . pas* (or other negative construction) goes around the pronoun and the verb together. Let's reconsider some sentences from above (in both the present and past tense) with negation:

*Elle **ne** la voit **pas** souvent.*	She doesn't see her often.
*Je **ne** te connais **pas** bien.*	I don't know you well.
*Je **ne** l'ai **pas** vue hier.*	I didn't see her yesterday.
*Il **ne** leur a **pas** parlé avant de venir.*	He didn't talk to them before coming.

Remember that, as you can see in those last two sentences, the negation only goes around the auxiliary verb in the *passé compose*.

Work with it

A. Underline the object pronouns in the sentences below and think about the differences in placement.

1. Je les vois souvent./Je les ai souvent vus./Je les voyais souvent.
2. Ils leur donnent de l'argent./Ils leur ont donné de l'argent./Ils leur donnaient de l'argent.
3. Tu me téléphones trop./Tu m'as trop téléphoné./Tu me téléphonais trop.
4. Nous la choisissons./Nous l'avons choisie./Nous la choisissions.
5. Elle lui parle tous les jours./Elle lui a parlé tous les jours./Elle lui parlait tous les jours.

B. Now for each of the translations below, choose the correct sentence from above and write it on the line.

1. I used to see them often. ____________________
2. They're giving them money. ____________________
3. You call me too much. ____________________
4. We chose it. ____________________
5. She used to talk to him every day. ____________________

B. Adverbial pronouns y *and* en

There are two more pronouns we need to address before moving on. They don't work the same way as direct and indirect object pronouns. Rather, they replace words that denote quantity, location, or objects of prepositional phrases. As with the pronouns we saw above, these go in front of the conjugated verb.

Y replaces prepositional phrases starting with *à* or other prepositions of location, such as *chez, dans, sur,* or *en*. It can be used to replace expressions of location or objects in prepositional phrases with *à*. Let's look at a few examples:

Je suis allé ***au marché****.*	I went to the market
*J'****y*** *suis allé.*	I went there.
Elle va rarement ***chez son frère****.*	She rarely goes to her brother's house.
Elle ***y*** *va rarement.*	She goes there rarely.
Tu penses souvent ***à tes choix****?*	Do you often think about your choices?
Tu ***y*** *penses souvent?*	Do you often think about it/them?

Note: *Y* is not used to refer to people, only to things. For example, in the sentence *Je pense souvent à mes parents,* the words *à mes parents* would be replaced with a disjunctive pronoun rather than *y*. This would result in the sentence *Je pense souvent à eux.*

En replaces a quantity, place, or object in prepositional phrases with *de*. Sometimes this is translated in English as "some," but many times it's left off entirely.

Vous voulez ***de la tarte aux pommes****?*	Would you like some apple pie?
Vous ***en*** *voulez?*	Would you like some?
Il a beaucoup ***de vêtements****.*	He has a lot of clothes.
Il ***en*** *a beaucoup.*	He has a lot (of them).
Tu te souviens ***de ton enfance****?*	Do you remember your childhood?
*Tu t'****en*** *souviens?*	Do you remember (about it)?

Note: As with *y, en* cannot be used to refer to people. So, for the question *Qu'est-ce que tu penses de ton patron?* ("What do you think of your boss?"), the disjunctive pronoun would again be used: *Qu'est-ce que tu penses de lui/d'elle?*

Work with it

A. In the following pairs of sentences, carefully read the question, identify the adverbial pronoun in the answer, and underline the prepositional phrase it refers back to.

1. Tu prends encore de la soupe? Non, je n'en prends pas.
2. Est-ce qu'il peut aller chez mon cousin? Oui, il peut y aller!
3. Pensent-elles souvent à leurs actions? Oui, elles y pensent souvent.
4. Vous avez beaucoup de travail à faire? Non, nous n'en avons pas beaucoup.
5. Il m'accompagne à la boulangerie, n'est-ce pas? Oui, il t'y accompagne.

B. Keeping in mind that translations in English will vary depending on sentence structure and verb choice, translate the first two questions and answers from exercise A.

1. ____________________
2. ____________________

C. Order of multiple pronouns

So what happens when more than one pronoun is needed? Here is a reference for the order of multiple pronouns in French:

me						
te	*le*	*lui*				
se	*la*	*leur*	*y*	*en*	+	verb
nous	*les*					
vous						

Consider, for example, the following sentence seen above:

*Je **lui** donne un cadeau.*   I give **her** a gift.

In this case, I've used the indirect object pronoun *lui* to replace "to him/to her."

Imagine that the original sentence was *Je donne un cadeau à mon ami*. I could just have easily used the direct object pronoun *le* to replace *un cadeau* instead.

*Je **le** donne à mon ami.*   I give **it** to my friend.

In typical language use, though, we frequently replace both the direct object and the indirect object with pronouns. Following the order above, it looks like this:

Je ***le lui*** *donne.* I give **it to him/to her**.

To become accustomed to seeing sentences with multiple direct and indirect object pronouns, study the following sentences:

Il ***me le*** *dit tous les jours.*	He says **it to me** every day.
Nous ***te les*** *offrons aujourd'hui.*	We offer **them to you** today.
Elle ***nous la*** *donne librement.*	She gives **it to us** freely.
Je ***la leur*** *envoie demain.*	I'm sending **it to them** tomorrow.

The adverbial pronouns *y* and *en* are always last in the order of object pronouns. You may, for instance, see something like:

Il ***y en*** *a beaucoup.*	**There**'s a lot (**of it**).
Je ***l'y*** *vois.*	I see **him there**.
Elle ***t'en*** *donne?*	Is she giving **you some**?

Past tense and negation: As is the case with one pronoun, so it is with multiple pronouns. The pronouns go before the auxiliary verb, and the negation goes around the pronouns and verb together. Let's go back to three of the sentences used above, and study how they would look in the *passé composé* and the present tense, both in the affirmative and the negative.

Present tense, affirmative

Nous ***te les*** *offrons aujourd'hui.*	We offer them to you today.
Elle ***nous la*** *donne librement.*	She gives it to us freely.
Je ***l'y*** *vois.*	I see him there.

Present tense, negative

Nous ***ne*** *te les offrons* ***pas*** *aujourd'hui.*	We don't offer them to you today.
Elle ***ne*** *nous la donne* ***pas*** *librement.*	She doesn't give it to us freely.
Je ***ne*** *l'y vois* ***pas****.*	I don't see him there.

Passé composé, affirmative

Nous ***te les*** *avons offerts aujourd'hui.*	We offered them to you today.
Elle ***nous l'****a donné librement.*	She gave it to us freely.
Je ***l'y*** *ai vu.*	I saw him there.

Passé composé, negative

Nous ***ne*** *te les avons* ***pas*** *offerts aujourd'hui.*	We didn't offer them to you today.
Elle ***ne*** *nous l'a* ***pas*** *donné librement.*	She didn't give it to us freely.
Je ***ne*** *l'y ai* ***pas*** *vu.*	I didn't see him there.

Work with it

What are the referents of the direct, indirect, and/or adverbial pronouns in the following past tense sentences? Follow the example to break them down. As you work, pay attention to the order of pronouns.

	Pronoun(s)	**Referent(s)**
Ex: Tu as vu ta grand-mère à la fête? Oui, je l'y ai vue.	l' (la), y	grand-mère, à la fête
1. Elle a parlé à sa mère de cela? Oui, elle lui en a parlé.	______	______
2. Vous êtes allés au supermarché? Oui, j'y suis allé.	______	______
3. Il a donné les jouets aux enfants? Oui, il les leur a donné.	______	______
4. Vous discutez de vos souvenirs? Oui, on en discute.	______	______
5. Il écrit une lettre à ses enfants? Oui, il la leur écrit.	______	______
6. Tu donnes les devoirs au prof? Oui, je les lui donne.	______	______

7 Ton mari a fait du pain pour toi? Oui, il m'en a fait. __________ ________________
8 Tu nous offres le livre? Oui, je vous l'offre. __________ ________________

IV. Reading and translation

Read the following dialogue from *Les plaisirs et les jours* by Marcel Proust (1896) and answer the questions below. (Note that many of the verbs are in the future tense, which you have not learned yet. Don't get too caught up in that; rather, concentrate on the pronouns. Once you've completed Chapter 10, come back and see how much more you can understand!)

"Monsieur Legrand, vaut-il mieux que mon oncle croie ou ne croie pas que je sais qu'il sait qu'il doit mourir?"
"Qu'il ne le croie pas, Alexis!"
"**Mais, s'il m'en parle?"**
"Il ne vous en parlera pas."
"Il ne m'en parlera pas?" dit Alexis étonné, car c'était la seule alternative qu'il n'eût pas prévue: Chaque fois qu'il commençait à imaginer sa visite à son oncle, il l'entendait lui parler de la mort avec la douceur d'un prêtre.
"Mais, enfin, s'il m'en parle?"
"Vous direz qu'il se trompe."
"Et si je pleure?"
"Vous avez trop pleuré ce matin, vous ne pleurerez pas chez lui."
"Je ne pleurerai pas!" s'écria Alexis avec désespoir, "mais **il croira que je n'ai pas de chagrin, que je ne l'aime pas** . . . mon petit oncle!"

1 Try to find the direct object, indirect object, or adverbial pronouns. How many are there? Can you figure out what they refer to?

2 What is happening to Alexis' uncle? What words give you this idea?

3 Translate the two phrases in bold, and check your answers in the back of the book. (The word *croira* is in the future tense, which you will learn in Chapter 10.)

8 Relative and interrogative pronouns

I. Funny French!

To start: You already know the question words *qui* and *que* from Chapter 2, along with how to form questions. This one is pretty easy to understand then, right?

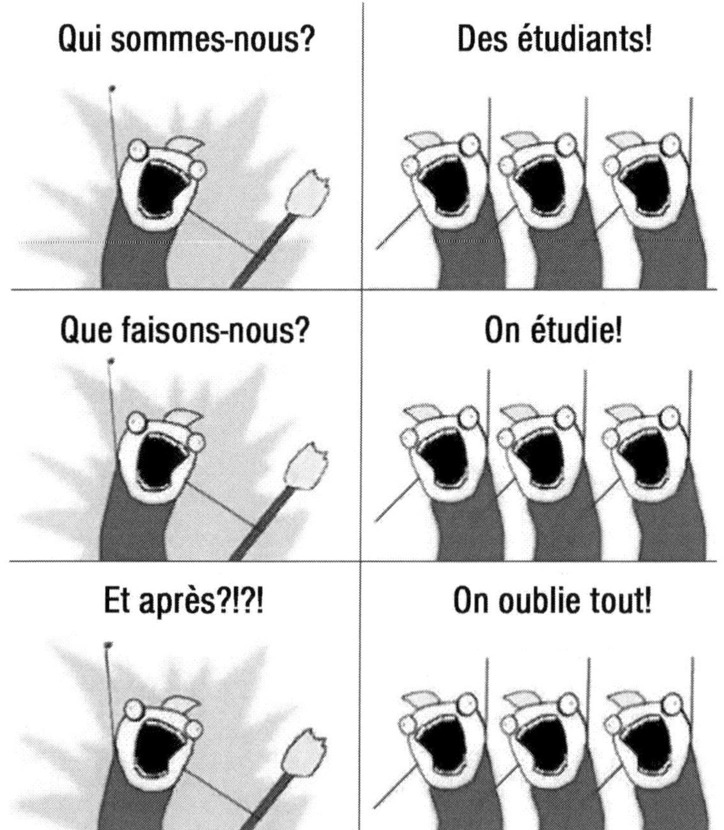

Qui sommes-nous?
Des étudiants!
Que faisons-nous?
On étudie!
Et après?!?!
On oublie tout!

Verify: Thinking back to subject pronouns, why do you think they used *on* in this context? Notice that even though it's being used to refer to a group of people (i.e. students), it's still conjugated as a third person singular subject.

II. Vocabulary

A. *Relative pronouns*

You may know that sentences can contain various combinations of independent and dependent clauses. Independent clauses can stand on their own as a sentence. Dependent clauses, on the other hand, cannot stand on their own and must be linked to the main (independent) clause using either a subordinating conjunction or a relative pronoun.

A relative clause is a type of dependent clause, one that gives more information about the noun that precedes it, and relative pronouns introduce these clauses. For instance:

The woman ***that* I saw yesterday** is quite beautiful.
Those are the shoes ***that* I wanted to buy**.
We are moving to Cincinnati, ***which* is my husband's hometown**.
Do you like the person ***who* gave you that sweater**?

French has several relative pronouns, and we will discuss how each of them is used in the Grammar section. For now, let's see what they look like, how they appear in sentences, and what their possible English counterparts are.

qui	*lequel*	*ce qui*
que	*laquelle*	*ce que*
dont	*lesquels*	*ce dont*
où	*lesquelles*	

I purposely left out translations in this list, because the way they correspond to English is highly dependent on the context of the sentence. So let's look at a few:

La dame ***qui travaille ici*** *est gentille.*	The woman **who works here** is nice.
Le gâteau ***que je fais*** *est délicieux.*	The cake **I'm making** is delicious.

*L'homme **dont je parle** arrive.*	The man **I'm talking about** is coming.
*Le théâtre **où nous jouons** est beau.*	The theater **where we perform** is beautiful.

In these sentences, you can see that I only translated two of the relative pronouns. Depending on the context, these French relative pronouns could be replaced in English by "who," "whom," "that," "where," or nothing. We'll talk about why this is the case later.

When used as relative pronouns, *lequel, laquelle, lesquels,* and *lesquelles* are used with prepositions and, as you might have guessed, they make agreement in gender and number with the noun that precedes them. Some prepositions you may see in front of these pronouns are *dans, parmi, entre,* and *pour.* Very often they are preceded by the preposition *à* or *de,* and when that is the case, they form a contraction as shown in this table:

	à	**de**
lequel	*auquel*	*duquel*
laquelle	*à laquelle*	*de laquelle*
lesquels	*auxquels*	*desquels*
lesquelles	*auxquelles*	*desquelles*

*La compagnie **pour laquelle il travaille** est grande.*	The company **he works for** is big.
*Les gens **parmi lesquels je me trouve** sont bons.*	The people **I find myself among** are good.
*La maison **dans laquelle ils vivent** me fait peur.*	The house **they live in** scares me.
*Le restaurant **près duquel j'habite** est excellent!*	The restaurant **I live close to** is excellent!
*La bague **à laquelle je me tiens le plus** est jolie.*	The ring **I'm most attached to** is pretty.

Ce qui, ce que, and *ce dont* function in the same way as *qui, que,* and *dont,* but are used when there isn't a specific referent in the sentence. You can see that these relative pronouns are frequently translated into English as "what."

Je suis étonnée par ***ce qu'*** *elle a dit.*	I'm stunned by **what** she said.
Elles ne comprennent pas ***ce qui*** *arrive.*	They don't understand **what**'s happening.
Tu sais que ce n'est pas ***ce dont*** *tu as besoin.*	You know that's not **what** you need.

Work with it

In the following sentences, identify the relative pronoun and write it on the line to the right.

1. Le truc dont j'ai peur, c'est le vide. ____________________
2. Explique-moi les raisons pour lesquelles il agit ainsi. __________
3. Je ne comprends pas du tout ce que tu fais. ______________
4. L'homme qui m'a donné ce cadeau est beau. _____________
5. C'est le groupe au sein duquel il s'est réfugié. ____________
6. Elle sait ce qui m'énerve le plus au monde. ______________
7. C'est la troupe de girafes que nous avons vue hier. _________

B. Interrogative pronouns

You were introduced to the French interrogative pronouns *qui* and *que* back in Chapter 2. They're pretty straightforward, meaning "who" and "what," respectively. In the Grammar section, we'll talk about how they can be combined with either *est-ce qui* or *est-ce que* in questions. For now, look at the table and sample sentences below to see how they are used.

	Subject of sentence	**Object of sentence**
qui	*Qui est-ce qui*	*Qui est-ce que*
que	*Qu'est-ce qui*	*Qu'est-ce que*

Qui est-ce qui *arrive demain?*	**Who**'s arriving tomorrow? (subject)
Qu'est-ce qui *t'énerve?*	**What** annoys you? (subject)
Qui est-ce que *tu aimes?*	**Whom** do you love? (object)
Qu'est-ce que *tu veux faire?*	**What** do you want to do? (object)

Note: The word *que* undergoes elision here, becoming *qu'* in front of the expression *est-ce que*, which starts with a vowel. To avoid confusion, *qui* never undergoes this process, so whenever you see *qu'*, you can be sure that it is the word *que*.

In part A, we looked at how the words *lequel, laquelle, lesquels,* and *lesquelles* combine with prepositions to act as relative pronouns in a sentence. Now we'll look at how these same words can be used on their own as interrogative pronouns, in which case they replace the interrogative adjective *quel* (*quelle, quels, quelles*) plus a noun.

Tu veux quel plat? Tu veux ***lequel****?*	You want which dish? You want which one?
Elle a acheté quelle bague? ***Laquelle****?*	She bought which ring? Which one?
Ils ont vu quels amis? ***Lesquels****?*	They saw which friends? Which ones?
Il aime quelles filles? Il aime ***lesquelles****?*	He likes which girls? He likes which ones?

Work with it

A. Which question is being asked below: "what" or "who/whom"? Is it the subject or the object of the sentence? Use the table above to help find the answers.

Ex: Qui est-ce qui t'a raconté cette histoire? What/Who(m) Subj/Obj

1. Qu'est-ce que tu aimes le plus chez ton mari? What/Who(m) Subj/Obj
2. Qui est-ce que le président a nommé? What/Who(m) Subj/Obj

3. Qui est-ce qui est le moins bien préparé? What/Who(m) Subj/Obj
4. Qu'est-ce qui vous donne cette impression? What/Who(m) Subj/Obj
5. Qu'est-ce qu'il a ordonné à ses employés? What/Who(m) Subj/Obj
6. Qui est-ce que vous préférez dans le concours? What/Who(m) Subj/Obj

B. Which noun is being referenced by the interrogative pronoun *lequel* (and its variants)?

Ex: Elle est allée au marché, mais je ne sais pas lequel. <u>le marché</u>

1. Je sais que tu aimes le vin, donc lequel devrais-je prendre? ____________
2. Il y avait beaucoup de fêtes. Tu es allé à laquelle? ____________
3. Parmi tous les invités, lesquels est-ce que tu connais? ____________
4. Lesquelles de ces voitures te semblent bonnes? ____________
5. J'aimerais un nouveau livre, mais je ne sais pas lequel. ____________

III. Grammar

A. Relative pronouns

To break down *qui, que, dont,* and *où,* let's revisit the sentences you saw in the Vocabulary section.

*La dame **qui travaille ici** est gentille.*	The woman **who works here** is nice.
*Le gâteau **que je fais** est délicieux.*	The cake **I'm making** is delicious.
*L'homme **dont je parle** arrive.*	The man **I'm talking about** is coming.
*Le théâtre **où nous jouons** est beau.*	The theater **where we perform** is beautiful.

Why did I use different relative pronouns in each of these sentences? Let's start with the first two sentences – in the first of them, the word *dame* is the subject of both the sentence and the relative clause. She is the woman who works here and she is also the woman who is nice. In this case, the English translation of the relative pronoun *qui* is "who." In the second sentence, however, the word *gâteau* is the subject of the sentence but it is the object of the relative clause. I'm making what? I'm making a cake. And that cake is delicious. In this case, the relative pronoun *que* is used, and the English equivalent is "that" (which I've dropped in the translation).

The relative pronoun *dont* is more complicated, but it basically translates to "of/about which" or "of/about whom." *Dont* can be hard for English speakers, because it has to do with a rule we frequently break. Even though we are not supposed to end sentences (or clauses) with prepositions, we do it all the time. We'll refer to "the person I'm going to school with" or we'll say "That's the person I was talking to you about." If we were to structure that last sentence to avoid the dangling preposition, we would say "That's the person about whom I was talking to you." This is essentially the function of *dont*. Any time a verb or expression ending in *de* is used, you'll find the word *dont*. Here are a few more examples:

parler de	*l'homme* ***dont*** *je te parlais*	the man I was talking to you **about**
avoir besoin de	*l'ingrédient* ***dont*** *il a besoin*	the ingredient he needs
avoir peur de	*la chose* ***dont*** *elle a peur*	the thing she's afraid **of**

Dont has two other functions. It is the equivalent of the English "whose" and can also be used to refer to members or parts of a larger group, as seen here:

C'est la femme ***dont*** *je connais le frère.*	That's the woman **whose** brother I know.
Voici l'homme ***dont*** *j'ai rencontré la femme.*	Here's the man **whose** wife I met.
Elle a des tas de livres, ***dont*** *le vôtre.*	She has many books, **including** yours.

Finally, *où* literally means "where," but it can also be used to talk about time.

Le parc ***où*** *les enfants jouent est très grand.*	The park **where** the children play is big.
Mercredi, c'est le jour ***où*** *je fais des recherches.*	Wednesday is the day I do research.
Le moment ***où*** *je l'ai vu, je savais.*	The moment I saw him, I knew.

These examples show that, as with other relative pronouns, *où* is sometimes translated into English as "where," and other times it's dropped entirely.

Now let's turn to *lequel, laquelle, lesquels,* and *lesquelles* as relative pronouns, looking again at the example sentences from above:

La compagnie ***pour laquelle il travaille*** *est grande.*	The company **he works for** is big.
Les gens ***parmi lesquels je me trouve*** *sont bons.*	The people **I find myself among** are good.
La maison ***dans laquelle ils vivent*** *me fait peur.*	The house **they live in** scares me.
Le restaurant ***près duquel j'habite*** *est excellent!*	The restaurant **I live close to** is excellent!
La bague ***à laquelle je me tiens le plus*** *est jolie.*	The ring **I'm most attached to** is pretty.

You'll notice that in each instance, the relative pronoun isn't translated. That's because we can (and often do) leave it out. It's also (again) because of our tendency to end clauses with a dangling preposition. Some would say that the fourth sentence should read "The restaurant close to which I live . . . ," a structure that necessitates the relative pronoun "(to) which." Since we ignore the preposition rule, though, we also drop the pronoun. Know that this is **not** possible in French, where you'll always see a relative pronoun and you'll never see a dangling preposition.

The relative pronouns *lequel, laquelle, lesquels,* and *lesquelles* agree in gender and number with their referent. In the first sentence above, the word *la compagnie* is feminine, so the pronoun *laquelle* is used. In the second sentence, *les gens* is masculine and plural, so *lesquels* is used.

Note: When using the various contracted forms of *auquel* to refer to a living being, *à qui* is possible as well. This is not possible for inanimate objects. For example:

La femme ***à qui*** *j'ai parlé hier . . .*	The woman I talked to yesterday . . .
Le chat ***à qui*** *j'ai donné à manger . . .*	The cat I fed . . .
Le garçon ***à qui*** *elle a offert son cadeau . . .*	The boy she offered her gift to . . .

Ce qui, ce que, and *ce dont* are called indefinite relative pronouns, and they are used in the same grammatical contexts as *qui, que,* and *dont.* The difference is that they appear in situations where there is no antecedent; that is, there is no prior noun in the sentence to which the pronoun obviously refers. In this case, the word *ce* stands in for that missing referent and the words *qui, que,* or *dont* function as normal.

Je ne comprends pas ***ce que tu dis****.*	I don't understand **what you're saying**.
Ce qui m'énerve*, c'est son attitude.*	**What annoys me** is her attitude.
Tu sais ***ce dont il a besoin****.*	You know **what he needs**.

You can see that these indefinite relative pronouns are most often translated into English as "what." They're also frequently used at the beginning of a sentence for emphasis, with the intended referent being added at the end of the sentence. For instance, the second sentence could have read *C'est son attitude qui m'énerve* ("It's her attitude that annoys me"). By leading with the indefinite relative pronoun, extra emphasis is added to the fact that I'm annoyed.

Work with it

Translate the sentences below, paying attention to whether to maintain the relative pronouns or drop them in English, and which words you use to translate them.

1. La ville près de laquelle nous habitons est souvent débordée de touristes.

   ____

2. Elle sait bien ce qui est nécessaire, mais elle hésite quand même.

___

3. Est-ce que vous vous souvenez de la famille dont je vous parlais?

___

4. Je m'en souviens bien. C'est le moment où je suis tombée amoureuse de lui.

___

5. J'ai vraiment apprécié l'humour des gens auxquels j'ai parlé à la fête hier soir.

___

6. Ce que je veux savoir, c'est comment elle a réussi à obtenir son diplôme.

___

B. Interrogative pronouns

Since you'll be reading French rather than speaking it, you don't have to make quite the same effort to distinguish among these four interrogative expressions. The most important thing to know is that the first word tells you what is being asked ("who(m)" or "what"). Returning to the examples from above:

Qui *est-ce qui arrive demain?*	**Who**'s arriving tomorrow? (subject)
Qu'*est-ce qui t'énerve?*	**What** annoys you? (subject)
Qui *est-ce que tu aimes?*	**Whom** do you love? (object)
Qu'*est-ce que tu veux faire?*	**What** do you want to do? (object)

The first and third sentences are asking "who" or "whom," while the second and fourth are asking "what" (with elision changing *que* to *qu'*).

The *qui* or *que* that comes after *est-ce que* has a grammatical function, letting you know whether that first question word is the subject or object of the question:

Qui est-ce ***qui*** *arrive demain?*	Who's arriving tomorrow? (**subject**)
Qu'est-ce ***qui*** *t'énerve?*	What annoys you? (**subject**)

Qui est-ce ***que*** *tu aimes?*	Whom do you love? (**object**)
Qu'est-ce ***que*** *tu veux faire?*	What do you want to do? (**object**)

Qui is used when the question word at the beginning of the sentence is the subject and *que* is used when the question word is the object. You can see this more clearly if we take the last two sentences and rearrange them:

Tu aimes ***qui****?*	You love **whom**?
Tu veux faire ***quoi****?*	You want to do **what**?

As I mentioned earlier, the *lequel* pronouns replace the interrogative adjective *quel* plus a noun. They translate to "which one" or "which ones," and they must agree in gender and number with the noun that is being replaced. For example, the following nouns would be replaced like this:

quel sujet? lequel?	which subject? which one?
quelle image? laquelle?	which picture? which one?
quels fromages? lesquels?	which cheeses? which ones?
quelles fenêtres? lesquelles?	which windows? which ones?

Even though *lequel* as an interrogative pronoun is often found without prepositions, as in the examples above, it can still be used with prepositions (and their corresponding contractions) if the verb and/or context requires it.

J'ai travaille au café hier.	I worked at the café yesterday.
Auquel?	(At) which one?
Il parle de ses souvenirs d'enfance.	He's talking about his childhood memories.
Desquels?	(About) which ones?
Nous parlons souvent à nos cousins.	We often talk to our cousins.
Auxquels?	(To) which ones?

Work with it

A. Complete the questions below by matching the interrogative pronoun on the left to the phrase on the right that makes the most sense logically and grammatically.

1. Qu'est-ce que . . . a. . . . te plaît?

2. Qu'est-ce qui . . . b. . . . tu as vu la semaine dernière?

3. Qui est-ce que . . . c. . . . vous faites ce soir?

4. Qui est-ce qui . . . d. . . . n'y est pas allé?

B. Now translate the questions from exercise A.

1. ________________________________

2. ________________________________

3. ________________________________

4. ________________________________

C. Fill in the sentences below with the interrogative pronoun that matches the noun in gender and number: *lequel, laquelle, lesquels,* or *lesquelles.*

1. Il a visité trois maisons, mais il ne sait pas encore ___________ il veut acheter.

2. Vous avez préparé plusieurs plats, mais ______________ sont les vôtres?

3. Ta soeur a reçu beaucoup de messages, alors ______________ as-tu écrit?

IV. Reading and translation

Read the following excerpt from *L'histoire du chevalier d'Iberville* by Adam-Charles-Gustave Desmazures (1890), then answer the questions below.

> Pour bien connaître ces temps de transition, **où** la petite colonie du Saint-Laurent atteignit l'étendue d'une domination presque aussi vaste que l'Europe, **il faut commencer par étudier quelques-uns des hommes d'État** et des hommes de guerre qui ont eu part à ces changements extraordinaires.
>
> Or, incontestablement, l'homme **dont** il faudrait d'abord s'occuper, c'est celui **qui** a été le plus remarquable de tous, celui **qui** a eu la vie la plus aventureuse et la destinée la plus glorieuse, **qui** a joué le rôle le plus éminent, pendant trente ans, dans les plus grands

événements du pays. Celui-là, **c'est l'illustre chevalier d'Iberville, de la famille des Le Moyne**; et nous croyons qu'il serait indispensable de le faire connaître avant tous.

D'Iberville était né à Montréal, en 1662, dans la maison de son père, Charles Le Moyne, sur la rue Saint-Joseph, **où** se trouve actuellement le bureau de la Fabrique de l'église Notre-Dame. Il a eu la gloire d'être associé aux plus grands évènements de ces premières années, et **on peut dire qu'il y a eu la part principale**.

1 After a first reading of this text, why might the chevalier d'Iberville be considered a great man (***Hint***: Look for the superlative construction)?

2 Look at the relative pronouns I've highlighted in bold. For each one, what subject is involved? What extra information is given about it?

3 Translate the phrases in bold and check your answers in the back of the book.

____

____

____

____

Demonstrative, possessive, and disjunctive pronouns

I. Funny French!

To start: The joke below contrasts the actions of *mon coeur* (my heart) and *ma conscience* (my conscience). Can you figure out how they do things differently?

Mon cœur oublie ceux qui l'offensent... mais ma conscience fait quand même une liste...

Verify: The word *ceux* in this joke is a demonstrative pronoun (masculine, plural) referring to people who do the following verb. You might also recognize the direct object pronoun *l'* (masculine, singular) in the word *l'offensent*. This refers back to *mon coeur*. Does this help you understand the joke? Check the back of the book to verify the meaning.

II. Vocabulary

A. Demonstrative pronouns

As with all pronouns, demonstrative pronouns function by replacing either a stated or implied noun, and they are used to *demonstrate* which person or thing is being mentioned ("this one," "that one," etc.). They agree in gender and number with the noun they replace.

Here's a list of the French demonstrative pronouns, with masculine in the top row and feminine in the bottom row:

celui	this one/that one	*ceux*	these/those
celle	this one/that one	*celles*	these/those

C'est une bonne tarte, mais il préfère ***celle*** *de sa mère.*
It's a good pie, but he prefers his mother's (literally: **the one/that** of his mother).

Entre les deux films, nous avons choisi ***celui*** *que je préfère.*
Between the two movies, we chose **the on**e that I prefer.

Tu vois cette voiture? C'est ***celle*** *dont je te parlais hier.*
You see that car? It's **the one** I was talking to you about yesterday.

Quand vous considérez les projets, n'oubliez pas ***ceux*** *de notre comité.*
When you consider the proposals, don't forget **those** of our committee.

Similarly to what we already saw with demonstrative determiners, the suffixes *-ci* and *-là* can be added directly to demonstrative pronouns to express relative proximity to the speaker. These are typically associated with choices.

Est-ce que tu préfères ***celle-ci ou celle-là****?*	Do you prefer **this one or that one**?
Quels plats voulez-vous, ***ceux-ci ou ceux-là****?*	Which dishes do you want, **these or those**?
Je ne sais pas si j'ai vu ***celui-ci ou celui-là****.*	I don't know if I saw **this one or that one**.

Work with it

For each sentence below, identify the demonstrative pronoun and use its gender and number to underline the noun (on the left) to which it refers.

1. Penses-toi que ta mère aimerait ce cadeau-ci ou celui-là?
2. J'aime cette actrice, mais j'adore celle qui joue dans mon film préféré.
3. Il préfère ces chaussures-ci parce que celles-là lui font mal aux pieds.
4. Tu as vu cette image? C'est celle qui te fait peur?
5. Elle choisit les tableaux modernes au lieu de ceux qui sont trop traditionnels.

B. *Possessive pronouns*

Similarly to what we saw with possessive determiners in Chapter 4, possessive pronouns are slightly more complicated because you have to consider both who is doing the possessing and whether the object that is possessed is masculine or feminine and singular or plural. Another particularity of French possessive pronouns is that they require a matching definite article, as seen in this table.

Singular		Plural		English
Masculine	**Feminine**	**Masculine**	**Feminine**	
le mien	*la mienne*	*les miens*	*les miennes*	mine
le tien	*la tienne*	*les tiens*	*les tiennes*	yours
le sien	*la sienne*	*les siens*	*les siennes*	his/hers/its
le nôtre	*la nôtre*	*les nôtres*	*les nôtres*	ours
le vôtre	*la vôtre*	*les vôtres*	*les vôtres*	yours
le leur	*la leur*	*les leurs*	*les leurs*	theirs

J'ai vu sa nouvelle maison, mais je préfère ***la mienne****.*
I saw his/her new house, but I prefer **mine**.

Il a déjà acheté ses livres pour la classe – as-tu ***les tiens****?*
He already bought his books for the class – do you have **yours**?

Nous voyons nos parents chaque samedi. Voyez-vous souvent ***les vôtres****?*
We see our parents every Saturday. Do you see **yours** often?

Notre chien est très gentil mais ***le leur*** *est méchant.*
Our dog is very nice but **theirs** is mean.

Work with it

Given the highlighted determiner and noun in each sentence, and using the table above, find the right possessive pronoun to replace it.

Ex: Ce sont mes trois petits chiens. les miens

1. Il est follement amoureux de **sa femme**. ________________
2. Elles réorganisent souvent **leurs meubles**. ________________
3. Nous avons du mal à trouver **notre certificat**. ________________
4. Tu vois souvent **tes anciennes élèves**? ________________
5. Où est-ce que vous avez trouvé **votre écharpe**? ________________
6. J'ai tendance à ronger **mes ongles**. ________________

C. Disjunctive pronouns

Disjunctive pronouns, sometimes called stressed pronouns, are personal pronouns that are used both for emphasis and in certain positions in a sentence. They are typically found either at the end of a prepositional phrase or at the beginning of a sentence followed by a comma, and correspond to the following English equivalents:

moi	me	*nous*	us
toi	you	*vous*	you
lui/elle/soi	him/her/oneself	*eux/elles*	them

They can also be combined with the word *même* ("same") for extra emphasis.

Je le fais ***moi-même****.*
I'm doing it **myself**.
Nous rentrons chez ***nous****.*
We're going to our house (literally: the house of **us**)
Et ***toi****, tu penses aux vacances?*
And **you**, are you thinking about vacation?
Tu veux aller avec ***eux****?*
Do you want to go with **them**?
C'est ***lui*** *qui a fait des bêtises.*
He's the one who did something stupid. (literally: it's **him** who . . .)
Elle pense souvent à ***vous****.*
She thinks of **you** often.
Tu es fatigué? ***Moi*** *aussi!*
You're tired? **Me** too!

Work with it

Circle the disjunctive pronoun in each of the sentences below, then write its English counterpart on the line to the right.

1. Tu n'aimes pas les olives? Lui non plus! ____________________
2. C'est bien elle qui a changé le système d'enregistrement. ________
3. Il vient de me dire qu'il pense souvent à toi. ______________
4. Les enfants peuvent faire la vaisselle eux-mêmes. ____________
5. Moi, je voudrais aller à la plage ce weekend. ______________

III. Grammar

A. Demonstrative pronouns

Demonstrative pronouns can take the place of either a demonstrative determiner and its noun or a noun in front of a prepositional phrase indicating possession.

Tu préfères ***cette chemise-ci****?*	Do you prefer **this shirt**?
Tu préfères ***celle-ci****?*	Do you prefer **this one**?
Elle a choisi ***ces chaussures-là****.*	She chose **those shoes**.
Elle a choisi ***celles-là****.*	She chose **those (ones)**.
J'adore ***la recette*** *de ma mère.*	I love my mom's **recipe**.
J'adore ***celle*** *de ma mère.*	I love my mom's (recipe).

Demonstrative pronouns are often found before a relative pronoun:

Je ne sais pas si c'est le bon bâtiment; c'est ***celui qui*** *se trouve entre l'école et la poste.*
I don't know if it's the right building; it's **the one** between the school and the post office.
Regarde ces articles; ce sont ***ceux dont*** *tu me parlais l'autre jour.*
Look at these articles; they're **the ones** you were talking to me about the other day.
Il t'a donné l'armoire? C'est ***celle dont*** *sa mère est si fière.*
He gave you the wardrobe? It's **the one** his mom is so proud of.

They are also frequently used to present a choice between two things:

Pour aller à la fête, est-ce que je devrais porter ***cette robe-ci ou celle-là****?*
To go to the party, should I wear **this dress or that one**?
Entre les deux chiens, lequel préfères-tu? ***Celui*** *avec les taches ou* ***celui*** *qui est petit?*
Between the two dogs, which one do you prefer? **The one** with spots or **the little one**?
Elles ne sont pas sûres quels endroits visiter – ***ceux-ci ou ceux-là****.*
They're not sure which places to visit – **these (ones) or those (ones)**.

Work with it

A. In the following sentences, underline the demonstrative determiner and its noun as well as the corresponding demonstrative pronoun (including any suffixes or other necessary words).

Ex: Ce n'est pas cet ordinateur-ci qu'il veut acheter, c'est celui qu'il a vu hier.

1. Nous avons décidé de soutenir cette association caritative au lieu de celle-là.
2. Tu partages ces recettes dans le livre? Je vais offrir celles de mon père.
3. Aide-moi! Est-ce que je devrais prendre ce plat-ci ou celui-là?
4. Je n'aime pas trop ces chemisiers – je préfère ceux dans l'autre magasin.

B. Now go back and translate the underlined parts of the sentences above.

Ex: this computer (here), the one he saw yesterday

1. ______________________________
2. ______________________________
3. ______________________________
4. ______________________________

B. Possessive pronouns

As you might remember from Chapter 4, the most difficult part of interpreting possessives is remembering that it's the gender and number of the thing that is possessed that matters for agreement, and not that of the possessor. The same is true for possessive pronouns, except that now you have a definite article added into the equation. To break this down, let's use a couple of examples that are similar, but not quite identical, to those from the Vocabulary section:

> *Il aime ma nouvelle maison, mais il préfère* ***la sienne***.
> He likes my new house, but he prefers **his**.

Correctly interpreting "his" or "her" is perhaps the most difficult, because the person could be masculine or feminine and so could the object. Here, the object being possessed is a house, *maison*, which is feminine. For that reason, the feminine article *la* is used, as well as the feminine form of the possessive pronoun, *sienne*. The person who possesses the house, however, is masculine, so it's translated into English as "his."

> *Nous aimons bien nos voisines, mais notre chien est très gentil alors que **le leur** est méchant.*
> We like our neighbors, but our dog is very nice while **theirs** is mean.

In this sentence, we know that the neighbors are women (*voisines* instead of *voisins*). Nevertheless, the word *chien* is masculine. This means that in order to refer to their dog, we use the definite article *le* and the word *leur* for "theirs."

Here are a few more examples so you can get accustomed to interpreting these sentences:

> *J'ai retrouvé mes amis au cinéma, mais je n'ai pas vu **les tiens**.*
> I met up with my friends at the movies, but I didn't see **yours**.
> *La recette de ma mère ne marche pas aussi bien que **la mienne**.*
> My mom's recipe doesn't work as well as **mine**.
> *Ils amènent toujours leurs enfants alors que **les nôtres** restent à la maison.*
> They always bring their kids while **ours** stay at home.
> *J'adore mon nouveau projet de travail – vous aimez **le vôtre**?*
> I love my new work project – do you like **yours**?
> *Mes collègues pensent que mes étudiants sont moins intelligents que **les leurs**.*
> My colleagues think my students are less intelligent than **theirs**.
> *Ma meilleure amie dit souvent que ma carrière est plus intéressante que **la sienne**.*
> My best friend often says that my career is more interesting than **hers**.

Work with it

Read the text below and identify all the possessive pronouns you see, then write them out and give their English translation below.

> Un jour, il y a deux semaines, Clara s'est rendu compte que son four ne marchait plus. Elle a donc téléphoné à son ami

Alain puisqu'il avait remplacé le sien le mois dernier. "Pourrais-tu venir voir le mien et me donner des conseils," a-t-elle demandé. Quand il est arrivé chez elle, il lui a dit, "J'ai oublié mes lunettes. Pourrais-je emprunter les tiennes?" Clara n'avait pas la même ordonnance que la sienne, mais il pouvait voir quand même. Après avoir regardé le four, Alain a conclu que c'était le même type que celui de ses parents. "Je peux leur demander s'ils ont jamais eu un problème pareil avec le leur," a-t-il dit.

	French	**English**
1.	________________	________________
2.	________________	________________
3.	________________	________________
4.	________________	________________
5.	________________	________________

C. Disjunctive pronouns

To fully understand the various ways disjunctive pronouns can be used, let's look at some examples of the various contexts in which you'll see them.

After a prepositional phrase

Je ne peux pas vivre ***sans lui****.*	I can't live **without him**.
Tu ne le fais pas ***pour eux****?*	You're not doing it **for them**?

In short answers

Moi *aussi!*	**Me** too!
Toi*!*	**You**!

In compound subjects

Mon mari et ***moi*** *sommes heureux.*	My husband and **I** are happy.
Toi *et* ***lui*** *partez?*	**You** and **he** are leaving?

For emphasis and to mean "self"

*Il n'est pas sûr, **lui**.*	**He**'s not sure.
*Tu l'aimes? Je l'ai fait **moi-même**.*	You like it? I made it **myself**.

After *c'est* and *ce sont*

*C'est **lui** qui a créé le problème.*	**He** created the problem. (He's the one who . . .)
*Ce sont **eux** qui viennent demain.*	**They**'re coming tomorrow.

Comparisons

*Il chante mieux que **moi**.*	He sings better than **me**.
*Je gagne moins que **lui**.*	I make less than **him**.

Possession

*Ce livre est à **elle**.*	This is **her** book.
*C'est ma veste à **moi**.*	It's **my** jacket.

Work with it

A. Can you distinguish between subject pronouns, object pronouns (direct and indirect), and disjunctive pronouns? Read the sentences below, identify each type of pronoun, and sort them into categories using the table below.

1. Il ne voulait pas lui parler de nous.
2. Moi, je préfère le faire tout au début.
3. Nous leur avons dit que c'était son manteau à elle.
4. Tu les as achetés toi-même?

	Subject pronoun	Object pronoun	Disjunctive pronoun
1.			
2.			
3.			
4.			

B. Now translate the following sentences from the text above.

1. Il ne voulait pas lui parler de nous.

____

2. Nous leur avons dit que c'était son manteau à elle.

____

IV. Reading and translation

Read the following excerpt from *Discours de la méthode* by René Descartes (1637), and answer the questions below.

> Le bon sens est la chose du monde la mieux partagée; car chacun pense en être si bien pourvu, que **ceux même qui sont les plus difficiles à contenter en toute autre chose** n'ont point coutume d'en désirer plus qu'ils en ont. En quoi il n'est pas vraisemblable que tous se trompent: mais plutôt cela témoigne que la puissance de bien juger et distinguer le vrai d'avec le faux, qui est proprement ce qu'on nomme le bon sens ou la raison, est naturellement égale en tous les hommes; et ainsi que la diversité de nos opinions ne vient pas de ce que les uns sont plus raisonnables que les autres, mais seulement de ce que nous conduisons nos pensées par diverses voies, et ne considérons pas les mêmes choses. Car ce n'est pas assez d'avoir l'esprit bon, mais le principal est de l'appliquer bien. Les plus grandes âmes sont capables des plus grands vices aussi bien que des plus grandes vertus; et **ceux qui ne marchent que fort lentement** peuvent avancer beaucoup davantage, s'ils suivent toujours le droit chemin, que ne font **ceux qui courent** et qui s'en éloignent.

1 If you have trouble with this text, don't worry! It contains some very abstract, philosophical musings. What cognates are you able to find? Do you see some structures you've already learned, e.g. comparatives and superlatives, object pronouns, and relative clauses?

2 The nice thing about this type of text is that most of the verbs are in the present tense. Are you able to understand most of the subject/verb

combinations, even though the gist of the sentences themselves might still be opaque?

3 We have three examples of demonstrative pronouns in this text. Can you translate the highlighted portions?

10 Future tense and conditional mood

I. Funny French!

To start: You'll need to know that the expression *faire semblant* means "to pretend." (There's a French verb *prétendre*, but it's a *faux ami* that means "to claim" or "to assert.") There are also two verbs in the future tense in this joke. Can you guess which ones they are? (***Hint***: It's definitely not the ones that are in the infinitive, or unconjugated form.)

Tant que
mon ***patron***
fera semblant
de ***bien*** me ***payer***
je ***ferai*** semblant
de bien
travailler

Verify: Check the meaning in the back of the book. This one was pretty easy, right? Notice that there's also a direct object pronoun in this sentence – can you find it? What does it refer to?

II. Vocabulary

Expressions of time

In Chapter 5, I introduced you to several expressions of time that are used to talk about things in the past tense. Now let's look at some vocabulary you're likely to see when reading about things in the future tense.

après-demain	the day after tomorrow
aussitôt	as soon as
bientôt	soon
demain	tomorrow
dès que	as soon as
dorénavant	from now on
lorsque	when
quand	when

You'll also need to recognize words and phrases that refer to the relation of events in time. Two important words to know are *prochain* (next) and *dernier* (last). As is the case with other adjectives, these have different forms based on the gender and number of the noun they modify, as seen in the table.

Masculine singular	Feminine singular	Masculine plural	Feminine plural
prochain	*prochaine*	*prochains*	*prochaines*
dernier	*dernière*	*derniers*	*dernières*

The position of the words *prochain* and *dernier* changes the meaning, so it's important to know how this works. If either of these words comes *before* the noun, you can go ahead and translate it directly from English:

la ***prochaine*** *année*	the next year
la ***dernière*** *semaine*	the last week
le ***dernier*** *mois*	the last month

In this case, the speaker could be referring to the last of a series, the last month of a job, the last day of a vacation, etc. They could also be specifying a time in relation to another event that's been mentioned: "I got promoted and the next year I left," for example.

If *prochain* or *dernier* comes *after* the noun, however, the time frame referenced is in relation to the present moment. In English, this generally means dropping the definite article:

l'année ***prochaine***	next year
la semaine ***dernière***	last week
le mois ***dernier***	last month

Speaking of weeks, months, and years, here is some basic vocabulary related to time.

une seconde	a second
une minute	a minute
une heure	an hour
une fois	one time
un jour/une journée	a day
une semaine	a week
un mois	a month
un an/une année	a year
aujourd'hui	today
demain	tomorrow
(et) demi	and a half
hier	yesterday
l'avant-hier	the day before yesterday
le lendemain	the next day
la veille	the night before/eve

Work with it

A. Based on the context of the sentence, which time word makes the most sense? Complete each sentence with a word from the list directly above, including the article.

1. Demain on dinera à notre restaurant préféré; __________ je serai sûrement malade.
2. Ça fait __________ qu'ils sont en couple; c'est leur anniversaire aujourd'hui.
3. J'ai passé __________ affreuse! Heureusement que c'est le weekend!
4. Nous adorons aller à la messe pour célébrer __________ de Noël.

B. Read these sentences carefully and decide how *prochain* or *dernier* is being used. Translate that portion to the right, following the model.

Ex: C'est la dernière fois que je l'ai vue. — the last time

1. Il cherchera un nouveau poste le mois prochain. ____________________
2. Aujourd'hui c'est le dernier jour de mes vacances. ____________________
3. L'année dernière elle a trouvé l'homme de sa vie. ____________________
4. Je serai indisponible pendant les dix prochains jours. ____________________
5. Il finira ses études l'année prochaine. ____________________

III. Grammar

A. *Future*

There are two ways to refer to future events in French: the *futur proche* (near future) and the *futur simple*. These correspond to the English expressions "am going to verb" and "will verb."

Futur proche is used to talk about events that are happening in the near future and that are fairly certain to happen. It is similar to the English construction for near future events in that it is formed by combining the verb *aller* (to go) with the infinitive form of the main verb.

*Ce soir **je vais sortir** avec mes amis.*	Tonight, **I'm going to go out** with my friends.
***Elle va acheter** du pain pour moi.*	**She's going to buy** some bread for me.
***Vous allez chanter** avec nous?*	**Are you going to sing** with us?
***Ils vont nous aider** à déménager.*	**They're going to help us** move.

Futur simple is used to talk about events that are further in the future and that may or may not be entirely certain: big-picture plans, for instance. This type of future is formed by adding specific endings to the infinitive form of the verb in question.

je	*-ai*	*nous*	*-ons*
tu	*-as*	*vous*	*-ez*
il/elle/on	*-a*	*ils/elles*	*-ont*

*Je t'**attendrai** en Europe.*	I **will wait for** you in Europe.
*Nous **fêterons** notre anniversaire.*	We **will celebrate** our birthday.
*Ils **choisiront** un nouveau président.*	They **will choose** a new president.
*Tu me **donneras** de l'argent?*	You **will give** me (some) money?
*Elle **dansera** dans la rue.*	She **will dance** in the streets.
*Vous **finirez** le projet cet été?*	You **will finish** the project this summer?

Notice that in the first sentence, there's actually one small spelling change. Verbs whose infinitive ends in *-re* drop the letter *-e* before the stem is added in the future tense (and the conditional mood). This is because it isn't necessary and would lead to an awkward combination of vowels.

Several common verbs have an irregular stem for the future tense, and in many cases they look nothing like the original verb. Here are a few you should be able to recognize:

aller	*ir-*	*faire*	*fer-*
avoir	*aur-*	*pouvoir*	*pourr-*
devoir	*devr-*	*savoir*	*saur-*
être	*ser-*	*vouloir*	*voudr-*

Nous ***irons*** *en France l'année prochaine.*	We **will go** to France next year.
Il ***aura*** *quinze jours de congé.*	He **will have** fifteen vacation days.
Tu ***pourras*** *nous rejoindre?*	**Will** you **be able** to join us?
Elles ***devront*** *travailler.*	They **will have** to work.
Je ***ferai*** *de mon mieux!*	I **will do** my best!

There's an important difference between French and English that you need to be aware of: when two related clauses are involved, both verbs are in the future tense. Check out the verbs in the following sentences in French and English. Do you see the difference?

Quand je ***serai*** *riche, je* ***voyagerai*** *souvent.*
When I **am** rich, I **will travel** often.
Nous ***aurons*** *plus de temps libre dès que nous* ***serons*** *diplômés.*
We **will have** more free time as soon as we **have** our degrees.
Il ***fera*** *du sport quand il en* ***aura*** *envie.*
He **will exercise** when he **feels like** it.
Lorsque vous ***trouverez*** *mon livre, vous me le* ***donnerez****?*
When you **find** my book, **you will** give it to me?

In French, since both actions will occur in the future, they are both conjugated in the future tense. Makes sense, right?

Object pronoun placement: Since we're talking about a compound tense (*futur proche*) and a simple tense (*futur simple*), we need to return to the issue of object pronoun placement. I said in Chapter 7 that object pronouns go in front of conjugated verbs, and that's true . . . a lot of the time. The exception is when you have a conjugated verb followed by an infinitive verb. This happens with verbs like *vouloir, pouvoir,* and *devoir,* which frequently need a second verb to complete an idea. It's also the case with the *futur proche.*

Ils veulent ***y*** *aller.*	They want to go (**there**).
Je dois ***lui*** *téléphoner.*	I have to call **him/her**.
Tu peux ***le*** *chercher au magasin?*	Can you get **it** at the store?
Nous allons ***l'****acheter.*	We are going to buy **it**.
Elle va ***en*** *parler demain.*	She's going to talk **about it** tomorrow.
Vous allez ***leur*** *donner un cadeau?*	Are you going to give **them** a gift?

You can see that in these cases, the object pronoun(s) goes *after* the conjugated verb and before the infinitive verb. If I conjugate those last three sentences in the *futur simple*, though, we return to a case where the pronoun is in front of the conjugated verb:

*Nous **l'**achèterons.*	We will buy **it**.
*Elle **en** parlera demain.*	She will talk **about it** tomorrow.
*Vous **leur** donnerez un cadeau?*	Will you buy **them** a gift?

Negation: This exception to object pronoun placement also affects negation. Let's return to the sentences I used above and look at the difference between *futur simple*, which follows the rules of negation we've discussed up to this point, and *futur proche*, which follows a different format.

*Nous **ne** l'achèterons **pas**.*	We will not buy it.
*Elle **n'**en parlera **pas** demain.*	She will not talk about it tomorrow.
*Vous **ne** leur donnerez **pas** un cadeau?*	Will you not buy them a gift?

*Nous **n'**allons **pas** l'acheter.*	We are not going to buy it.
*Elle **ne** va **pas** en parler demain.*	She's not going to talk about it tomorrow.
*Vous **n'**allez **pas** leur donner un cadeau?*	Aren't you going to give them a gift?

In the first set of sentences, we see the same negation format as with the present tense – that is, the *ne . . . pas* goes around both the conjugated verb and any object pronouns. In the second set of sentences, however, you can see that the negation goes around the verb *aller* and the object pronouns stay outside of the negative expression. The same goes for verbs like *vouloir*, *pouvoir*, and *devoir* which use a second verb in the infinitive:

*Ils **ne** veulent **pas** y aller.*	They don't want to go (there).
*Je **ne** dois **pas** lui téléphoner.*	I don't have to call him/her.
*Tu **ne** peux **pas** le chercher au magasin?*	Can't you get it at the store?

Work with it

A. In the following sentences, is the verb in *futur proche* (FP) or *futur simple* (FS)? How would you translate it into English?

	FP/FS	Translation
Ex: Elle fera bientôt partie de l'équipe.	FS	will be part
1. Les élèves vont rendre leurs devoirs.	________	________
2. Nous aurons du temps le mois prochain.	________	________
3. Il sera le meilleur joueur.	________	________
4. Tu vas promener le chien?	________	________
5. On va le voir dans une semaine.	________	________

B. In the following sentences, identify and underline the future tense verb(s), any pronouns, and the *ne . . . pas* if applicable. ***Hint***: There may be more than one verb in the future tense.

Ex: J'ai compris ta question mais je ne vais pas y répondre.

1. Nous les verrons quand ils nous rendront visite.
2. Tu vas en parler avec ta mère, ou est-ce qu'elle sera réticente?
3. Puisque je suis anxieuse, je ne parlerai pas lors de la conférence.
4. Il ne va pas la voir, même si elle s'excuse?

C. Now translate the sentences from exercise B.

1. ______________________________
2. ______________________________
3. ______________________________
4. ______________________________

B. Conditional

To be precise with our terms, future is a tense and conditional is a mood. That is to say, things that happen in the conditional mood are still happening in the future, but they are hypothetical rather than indicative. The conditional doesn't change *when* something happens, but *how*.

Formation: The conditional uses the same stems as the *futur simple*. For most verbs, this means the infinitive, but this stem sharing goes for all irregular verbs as well. This makes learning the future and conditional together fairly easy, but it can also lead to confusion in reading, because a slight change in endings is all you get to help you distinguish between the two forms. The endings for conditional are:

je	*-ais*	*nous*	*-ions*
tu	*-ais*	*vous*	*-iez*
il/elle/on	*-ait*	*ils/elles*	*-aient*

(You may recognize these endings from the imperfect in Chapter 5, and that's because they are exactly the same.)

*J'**aimerais** voir mes parents plus souvent.*	I would like to see my parents more often.
*Nous y **irions** s'il était possible.*	We would go there if it were possible.
***Pourrais**-tu le faire avec moi?*	Could you do it with me?
*Elle le **ferait** pour plus d'argent.*	She would do it for more money.

The conditional is most frequently seen in sentences using *si* clauses, or "if . . . then" statements. These are sentences that present a hypothetical situation (using the imperfect in French) along with the hypothetical result of that condition (in the conditional).

*Si nous gagnions à la loterie, nous **achèterions** une nouvelle maison.*
If we won the lottery, we **would buy** a new house.
*J'**aurais** plus de confiance en lui s'il me parlait davantage.*
I **would have** more faith in him if he talked to me more.
*Si le temps faisait beau, ils **feraient** de la planche à voile.*
If it were nice out, they **would go** windsurfing.

The conditional is also used to express politeness, especially with the verbs *aimer* and *vouloir*. Just as one says "I would like . . ." to order a meal in

English, one says "*Je voudrais . . .*" or "*J'aimerais*" in French. But it goes beyond these two verbs:

Auriez-vous des suggestions pour mon projet?	Do you have suggestions for my project?
Pourriez-vous[1] *me donner des renseignements?*	Could you give me some information?
Aimeriez-vous m'accompagner?	Would you like to accompany me?

Since conditional is a simple construction, it follows the typical rules for negation and object pronoun placement.

Je ***ne lui parlerais pas*** *dans ce cas-là.*	I **wouldn't speak to him** in that case.
Elles ***le leur donneraient*** *tout de suite.*	They **would give it to them** right away.
Il ***ne chanterait pas*** *devant un public.*	He **wouldn't sing** in front of an audience.
Vous ***n'en voudriez pas****?*	You **wouldn't like any**?

Work with it

A. How would you conjugate the short sentences below?

1. Il n'aimerait pas vendre sa maison. ______________________

2. Nous serions heureux de te voir. ______________________

3. Tu pourrais nous joindre demain? ______________________

B. Using what you know about sentences with *si* clauses as well as contextual clues, match the *si* clause on the left to the conditional clause on the right.

1. Si elle avait plus de temps libre . . .	**a.** . . . je n'en aurais pas trois.
2. Si nous voulions voyager avec eux . . .	**b.** . . . elle lirait plus de livres.
3. Si je n'aimais pas les chiens . . .	**c.** . . . elles ne seraient pas profs.

4. Si je travaillais plus dur . . . d. . . . nous le leur proposerions.
5. Si elles étaient moins intelligentes . . . e. . . . je finirais plus tôt.

C. Now let's see if you can keep track of how the stem/ending combinations overlap in the future, conditional, and imperfect. Look at the verbs in the following list and sort them into the right category in the table below.

tu parlais

ils auront

je donnerai

nous faisions

vous auriez

tu parlerais

ils auraient

elle donnait

on aura

Future	Conditional	Imperfect

IV. Reading and translation

Read the dialogue from *Le comte de Monte-Cristo* by Alexandre Dumas (1845), and answer the questions below.

"Il lui eût été impossible d'écrire, monsieur; mais cela me rappelle que j'aurai un congé de quinze jours à vous demander."

"Pour vous marier?"

"D'abord; puis pour aller à Paris."

"Bon, bon! **vous prendrez le temps que vous voudrez**, Dantès; le temps de décharger le bâtiment nous prendra bien six semaines, et nous ne nous remettrons guère en mer avant trois mois. . . . Seulement, dans trois mois, il faudra que vous soyez là. Le Pharaon, continua l'armateur en frappant sur l'épaule du jeune marin, ne pourrait pas repartir sans son capitaine."

"Sans son capitaine!" s'écria Dantès les yeux brillants de joie; "faites bien attention à ce que vous dites là, monsieur, car vous venez de répondre aux plus secrètes espérances de mon cœur. **Votre intention serait-elle de me nommer capitaine du Pharaon**?"

"Si j'étais seul, je vous tendrais la main, mon cher Dantès, et je vous dirais: 'C'est fait.' Mais j'ai un associé, et vous savez le proverbe italien: Che a compagne a padrone. Mais la moitié de la besogne est faite au moins, puisque sur deux voix vous en avez déjà une. Rapportez-vous-en à moi pour avoir l'autre, et **je ferai de mon mieux**."

1 What is Dantès asking of his superior? Why? What response does he get?
2 What does Dantès' superior offer him? Does this make Dantès happy? How do you know?
3 In the second highlighted phrase, why is the conditional used? Would we do that in English?
4 Translate the highlighted phrases, and check your answers in the back of the book.

____

____

____

____

Note

1 All verbs are conjugated the same way in the French conditional, so *pouvoir* and *devoir* can be difficult for English speakers since they are special cases for us (i.e. "could" and "should" instead of "would + verb").

11 Impersonal expressions and obligation

I. Funny French!

To start: You're probably familiar with this genre of joke, featuring cats who seem to have a bad attitude. You should also be able to recognize that a couple of the verbs are in the future tense. Pick out the words you can understand and see how much of the joke you can understand.

Vas-y, donne-moi n'importe quel nom ridicule. De toute façon, quand tu m'appelleras, je ne viendrai pas.

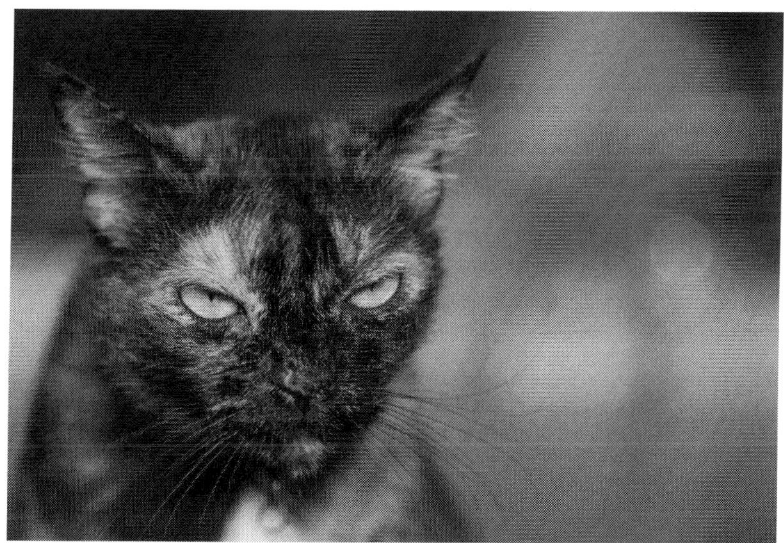

Verify: Check the translation in the back of the book, and identify the words you didn't know. One of the things we'll go over in this chapter is the imperative (commands), so by the end you'll have a better understanding of the first two verbs in this joke: *vas-y* and *donne-moi*.

II. Vocabulary

In this chapter you'll be introduced to impersonal expressions using the subject pronoun *il*, as well as both the subjunctive and the imperative to express obligation. To prepare, let's look at some of the impersonal expressions that are possible in these circumstances.

A. Common impersonal expressions

As you read in French, you'll come across uses of the pronoun *il* that don't seem to make sense when translated as "he." That's because French also uses this pronoun in impersonal expressions, where the actions and events described do not refer to a specific person. Two examples of this phenomenon are time (*Il est . . .*) and weather (*Il fait . . .*). This type of expression is usually translated into English as "it."

Let's start with the weather, since it has a couple different forms. Most descriptions of weather start with *Il fait*, as seen in the following sentences:

Il fait chaud. It's hot.
Il fait froid. It's cold.
Il fait beau. It's beautiful (outside).
Il fait orageux. It's stormy.

An important exception to this rule is that precipitation has its own verbs, so it doesn't use the verb *faire*. For example:

Il pleut. It's raining.
Il neige. It's snowing.
Il gèle. It's freezing.

There are also a couple of situations where the expression *il y a* ("there is/there are") is used:

Il y a du soleil.	It's sunny.
Il y a du brouillard.	It's foggy.
Il y a du vent.	It's windy.

Impersonal *il* is also used to tell time. You should know that when the time is written in French, the letter "h" is used instead of a colon. This stands for the word *heure* (hour). Another important thing to note is that French often uses the 24-hour clock. If the 24-hour clock is not used, then time of day will usually be specified in words.

Il est 1h10.	It's 1:10 a.m. (literally: it's one hour ten).
Il est midi.	It's noon.
Il est 16h30.	It's 4:30 p.m.
Il est 2h00 de l'après-midi.	It's 2:00 in the afternoon.
Il est 8h00 du soir.	It's 8:00 at night.
Il est 7h00 moins dix.	It's 6:50 a.m. (literally: it's 7:00 minus ten).

Aside from these specific uses, impersonal *il* is also used extensively to express obligation, to give opinions, and in idiomatic expressions. Here are some of the ways you're most likely to encounter impersonal *il* expressions:

Il arrive . . .	It happens . . .
Il s'agit de . . .	It's about . . ./It's a question of . . .
Il faut . . .	It's necessary . . .
Il manque . . .	To be missing . . .
Il semble . . .	It seems . . .
Il vaut mieux . . .	It's better . . .

Now consider a few sentences using the above expressions:

Il vaut mieux que tu viennes.	It's better that you come.
Il s'agit de savoir la réponse.	It's a question of knowing the answer.
Il me manque une chaussette.	I'm missing a sock.
Il semble qu'il est mal à l'aise.	It seems that he's uncomfortable.

You may also see impersonal *il* used with subordinate clauses in the following format:

Il est + adjective + *que*

This may occur in any number of the following types of sentences:

Il est clair que tu l'aimes.	It's clear that you love him/her/it.
Il est certain que nous y allons.	It's certain that we're going (there).
Il est important qu'il le fasse.	It's necessary that he do it.
Il est normal que tu aies peur.	It's normal that you're scared.
Il est urgent que vous en parliez.	It's urgent that you talk about it.
Il est vrai que je suis professeur.	It's true that I'm a teacher.

Work with it

A. Read the time and choose the activity that's most likely to happen then.

1. Il est midi.	**a.** On se réveille.
2. Il est 3h00 de l'après-midi.	**b.** On mange le dîner.
3. Il est 6h45.	**c.** On se couche.
4. Il est 23h00.	**d.** On rentre de l'école.
5. Il est 7h00 du soir.	**e.** On mange le déjeuner.

B. Given the context of the sentence (i.e. the activity or action described), circle the most logical weather expression to complete the sentence.

1. Nous sommes rentrés chez nous parce qu'il [pleut/fait beau].

2. S'il [fait du vent/fait orageux], on fera de la planche à voile.

3. Aujourd'hui je joue au tennis parce qu'il [fait froid/fait beau].

4. Ils préfèrent porter un manteau quand il [fait froid/fait chaud].

5. S'il [neige/fait du brouillard], les enfants joueront dehors.

C. Use context clues and the words you know to match the French sentence on the left to its English counterpart on the right.

1. Il est dommage qu'ils soient partis.	**a.** It's true that she works here.
2. Il est évident que tu es heureux.	**b.** These things happen often.

3.	Il est vrai qu'elle travaille ici.	**c.**	It's obvious that you're happy.
4.	Il semble que vous aimez le cinéma.	**d.**	It's good that you're not scared
5.	Il arrive souvent de telles choses.	**e.**	It's too bad they left.
6.	Il est bon que tu n'aies pas peur.	**f.**	It seems that you like film.

B. Impersonal expressions, verbs, and conjunctions that trigger the subjunctive

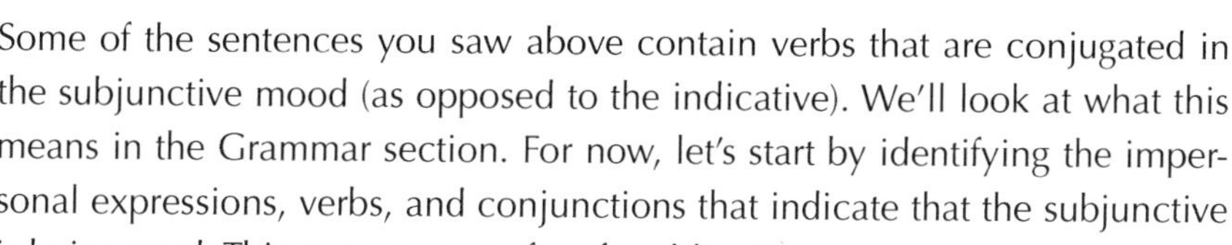

Some of the sentences you saw above contain verbs that are conjugated in the subjunctive mood (as opposed to the indicative). We'll look at what this means in the Grammar section. For now, let's start by identifying the impersonal expressions, verbs, and conjunctions that indicate that the subjunctive is being used. This occurs most often for obligation:

Obligation and preference: impersonal expressions

Il est essentiel que	it's essential that
Il est important que	it's important that
Il est nécessaire que	it's necessary that
Il est urgent que	it's urgent that
Il faut que	it's necessary that

Obligation and preference: verbs

commander que	to order that
exiger que	to require that
préférer que	to prefer that
souhaiter que	to wish that
vouloir que	to want that

In addition to the expression of obligation, the subjunctive is used with expressions of preference, doubt, emotion, and judgment, and with certain conjunctions.

Feelings and judgments: impersonal expressions

il est bon que	it's good that
il est dommage que	it's too bad that
il est regrettable que	it's regrettable that
il est surprenant que	it's surprising that

Feelings and judgments: verbs

avoir peur que	to be afraid that
détester que	to hate that
être [triste/heureux/surpris/etc.] que	to be [sad/happy/surprised/etc.] that
regretter que	to regret that

Doubt: impersonal expressions

il est douteux que	it's doubtful that
il est impossible que	it's impossible that
il semble que	it seems that
il se peut que	it may be that

Doubt: verbs

douter que	to doubt that
refuser que	to refuse that
supposer que	to suppose that

Conjunctions

à condition que	on the condition that
afin que	in order that/so that
bien que	although
de peur que	for fear that
jusqu'à ce que	until
pour que	so that
pourvu que	provided that
sans que	without

Work with it

A. Take the list of verbs and expressions in the box and organize them according to category: obligation, doubt, or feelings and judgments. There will be three in each category.

il faut que	douter que	exiger que
il est triste que	il n'est pas certain que	regretter que
il est impossible que	il vaut mieux que	il est surprenant que

Obligation	**Doubt**	**Feelings/judgments**
________	________	________
________	________	________
________	________	________

B. In the following short paragraph from *De la démocratie en Amérique* by Alexis de Tocqueville (1848), analyze the expressions that I've highlighted. These expressions may be new to you, but try to decipher their meaning and see if you can understand why they trigger the subjunctive.

Il me paraît hors de doute que tôt ou tard nous arriverons, comme les Américains, à l'égalité presque complète des conditions. **Je ne conclus point de là que** nous soyons appelés un jour à tirer nécessairement, d'un pareil état social, les conséquences politiques que les Américains en ont tirées. **Je suis très loin de croire qu'ils** aient trouvé la seule forme de gouvernement que puisse se donner la démocratie; mais **il suffit que** dans les deux pays la cause génératrice des lois et des mœurs soit la même, **pour que** nous ayons un intérêt immense à savoir ce qu'elle a produit dans chacun d'eux.

III. Grammar

The subjunctive in French is a very common way of expressing obligation or imposing one's will on someone else. This is why it's important to be able to recognize it when you see it, especially since it's rarely used in English. It's a rather complicated case, though, so we'll come back to it. First, let's look at a slightly easier way of expressing obligation: the imperative mood.

A. *Imperative*

I briefly touched on the difference between tense and mood in our Chapter 10 discussion of the conditional. Both imperative and subjunctive are moods. Whereas tense refers to the time something happened (past, present, future), mood refers to the manner. The mood we use most of the time, and which probably seems like the "normal" present tense to us, is the indicative. This mood means we are, well, *indicating* something.

Another mood we can use is the imperative. Here, instead of indicating something, we're demanding something. You'll only see this mood used in the present tense, since it refers to something being demanded in the present moment.

Formation: Imperative mood is the only time the subject pronoun can be dropped in French. You'll only see the imperative used with three subjects: *tu, vous*, and *nous*, because you obviously give commands directly to someone, rather than to third-person subjects, like "he" or "they." When *nous* is used in the imperative, it's usually a suggestion rather than a command.

Imperative is formed by dropping the subject pronoun and dropping the *-s* from the *tu* form for *-er* verbs and a small handful of *-ir* verbs. Here is a table showing the indicative and the imperative for each of the three verb groups:

-*er* verbs		**-*ir* verbs**		**-*re* verbs**	
Indicative	**Imperative**	**Indicative**	**Imperative**	**Indicative**	**Imperative**
tu regardes	*regarde!*	*tu finis*	*finis!*	*tu choisis*	*choisis!*
vous regardez	*regardez!*	*vous finissez*	*finissez!*	*vous choisissez*	*choisissez!*
nous regardons	*regardons!*	*nous finissons*	*finissons!*	*nous choisissons*	*choisissons!*

Note: Something to look out for when you see pronominal verbs (i.e. reflexive and reciprocal verbs) in the imperative, is that while the subject pronoun is dropped, the reflexive pronoun is retained. It moves position to follow the verb and takes a different form (resembling the disjunctive pronoun). So, for example, the indicative *tu te lèves* becomes *lève-toi* in the imperative, *vous vous lavez les mains* becomes *lavez-vous les mains*, etc.

There are four irregular verbs that use their subjunctive form for the imperative.

	avoir	être	savoir	vouloir
(tu)	*aie*	*sois*	*sache*	*veuille*
(vous)	*ayez*	*soyez*	*sachez*	*veuillez*
(nous)	*ayons*	*soyons*	*sachons*	*n/a*

Pronunciation note: Sometimes you'll see the *-s* added back onto a verb in the imperative. This is for the purpose of pronunciation, and occurs when a pronoun starting with a vowel is attached to the verb. For example, *vas-y* (go on) or *achètes-en* (buy some). You may also see pronouns change spelling depending on the attachment of additional pronouns. For example, *parlez-moi* (talk to me) becomes *parlez-m'en* (talk to me about it).

Negation: Because imperative sometimes involves inverting words, negating it can be more complicated than in the indicative. This isn't too much of a problem when no pronouns are involved, in which case the *ne . . . pas* goes around the verb as usual:

***Ne** chante **pas**!*	**Don't** sing!
***N'**ayez **pas** peur.*	**Don't** be afraid.
***Ne** parle **pas** comme ça.*	**Don't** talk like that.

Once reflexive or object pronouns are involved, though, the word order changes back to more of a typical sentence structure. Check out the following affirmative and negative commands, and notice their word order:

*Donne-le-moi./**Ne** me le donne **pas**.*	Give it to me./Don't give it to me.
*Parlez-lui/**Ne** lui parlez **pas**.*	Talk to him./Don't talk to him.
*Lave-toi les mains./**Ne** te lave **pas** les mains.*	Wash your hands./Don't wash your hands.

Note: *Nous* is also used in the imperative, but since it includes the speaker, it's usually interpreted as a suggestion rather than an order. For example, in *allons à la plage* (let's go to the beach), the sense of command is weaker than in *allez à la plage* (go to the beach).

Work with it

A. What would I say to people in the following situations? Match the situation with the appropriate command.

1. Ma fille ne veut pas manger ses légumes.	**a.** Sortez la poubelle!
2. Mon mari vient de rentrer et je veux lui parler.	**b.** Ecoute bien!
3. Un élève ne fait pas attention en classe.	**c.** Allons-y!
4. Les enfants doivent faire leurs tâches ménagères.	**d.** Mange-les!
5. Nous devons aller faire les courses.	**e.** Viens ici!

B. Translate the following commands into English.

1. Rends-le-lui! ____________________

2. Va ranger ta chambre! ____________________

3. Parle m'en. ____________________

4. Regardons un film. ____________________

5. Ecoute ton professeur! ____________________

B. Subjunctive

We've seen that while indicative is the most common mood in the present tense, orders are given using the imperative mood. Now we turn back to the subjunctive mood. The subjunctive can be a very thorny topic for those learning to speak French, since they have to master when to use it. It should be easier for you as a reader, because all you need to be able to do is recognize the subjunctive when it occurs and know why you're seeing it.

As I mentioned in the Vocabulary section, the subjunctive is used to indicate obligation, to cast doubt, and to express feelings, preferences, and judgments.

Formation: For regular verbs of all groups, the subjunctive is based on the third-person plural form. The ending is dropped, and the remaining letters are used as the stem. Here are the present subjunctive endings:

je	*-e*	*nous*	*-ions*
tu	*-es*	*vous*	*-iez*
il/elle/on	*-e*	*ils/elles*	*-ent*

Let's start by analyzing how this looks for a regular *-er* verb, like *parler* (to speak).

je parle	*nous parlions*
tu parles	*vous parliez*
il/elle on parle	*ils/elles parlent*

You'll notice that with the exception of *nous* and *vous*, which have an added *-i-*, these conjugations look the same as the indicative mood. Easy enough! Things look quite a bit different when we move to *-ir* verbs, however. Consider the verbs *finir* and *rendre*:

je finisse	*nous finissions*
tu finisses	*vous finissiez*
il/elle/on finisse	*ils/elles finissent*

je rende	*nous rendions*
tu rendes	*vous rendiez*
il/elle/on rende	*ils/elles rendent*

In *finir*, because we start from the double *-s-* in the third-person plural, the singular forms suddenly look quite different from their typical indicative form (*je finis, tu finis, il finit*). The third-person plural, however, looks the same. This is because it's used as the stem and has the same ending in both moods. This is also the case with *-er* and *-re* verbs, and the same thing happens with the *-d-* in *rendre*.

Pronunciation note: Not only do the singular forms of *-ir* and *-re* verbs *look* different than usual, they're pronounced quite differently as well. Their indicative forms end in consonants, which usually aren't pronounced in this position. *Finis*, for example, sounds like fee-nee. When the subjunctive form is used, a vowel follows the consonant, *finisse*, which leads to the consonant being pronounced. It now sounds like fee-neese.

Of course, what fun would it be if there weren't some irregular verbs to consider? A few of these irregular verbs simply have a different stem for *nous* and *vous* in the subjunctive.

aller	*j'aille*	*nous allions*
to go	*tu ailles*	*vous alliez*
	il/elle/on aille	*ils/elles aillent*
devoir	*je doive*	*nous devions*
to have to	*tu doives*	*vous deviez*
	il/elle/on doive	*ils/elles doivent*
prendre	*je prenne*	*nous prenions*
to take	*tu prennes*	*vous preniez*
	il/elle/on prenne	*ils/elles prennent*
venir	*je vienne*	*nous venions*
to come	*tu viennes*	*vous veniez*
	il/elle/on vienne	*ils/elles viennent*
vouloir	*je veuille*	*nous voulions*
to want	*tu veuilles*	*vous vouliez*
	il/elle/on veuille	*ils/elles veuillent*

Other irregular verbs have entirely different forms in the subjunctive, and these include many of the verbs that are irregular in other moods and tenses:

avoir	*j'aie*	*nous ayons*
to have	*tu aies*	*vous ayez*
	il/elle/on ait	*ils/elles aient*
être	*je sois*	*nous soyons*
to be	*tu sois*	*vous soyez*
	il/elle/on soit	*ils/elles soient*
faire	*je fasse*	*nous fassions*
to do/	*tu fasses*	*vous fassiez*
to make	*il/elle/on fasse*	*ils/elles fassent*
pouvoir	*je puisse*	*nous puissions*
to be able to	*tu puisses*	*vous puissiez*
	il/elle/on puisse	*ils/elles puissent*

savoir	*je sache*	*nous sachions*
to know	*tu saches*	*vous sachiez*
(how)	*il/elle/on sache*	*ils/elles sachent*

Work with it

A. See if you can find the three verbs in the subjunctive in the following short text. Write them on the lines below.

Bien qu'il soit malade, Benoit a décidé d'aller à l'école. Il voulait à tout prix voir son amour – sans qui il ne pourrait pas vivre – il était donc essentiel qu'il y aille. En arrivant en classe, il l'a vu tout de suite. Son coeur s'est mis à battre plus vite quand son amour lui a dit, "Je suis triste que tu ne te sentes pas bien, mon chéri."

________________ ________________ ________________

B. For each sentence below, decide whether the highlighted verb is in the subjunctive or the indicative mood. Give a brief explanation for this (e.g. necessity, doubt, emotion, or preference for the subjunctive, or certainty for the indicative). Note that #3 has two verbs to analyze.

1. Nous savons qu'il ne nous **dit** pas la vérité.
2. Vu la neige, il est douteux que nos amis **viennent** ce soir.
3. Je sais que tu **es** occupé, mais il est urgent que nous **allions** à l'hôpital.
4. Elles sont vraiment ravies que tu **viennes** à la soirée.
5. Le patron préfère que vous ne **partiez** pas en vacances cette semaine.

	Subjunctive or indicative?	**Reason?**
1.		
2.		
3.	a. b.	a. b.
4.		
5.		

IV. Reading and translation

Read the following dialogue from *La comédie humaine* by Honoré de Balzac (1874), and answer the questions below.

"Asseyez-vous là," lui dit Guillaume en lui désignant le tabouret.

Comme jamais le vieux maître-drapier n'avait fait asseoir son commis devant lui, Joseph Lebas tressaillit.

"Que pensez-vous de ces traites?" demanda Guillaume.
"Elles ne seront pas payées."
"Comment?"
"Mais j'ai su qu'avant-hier Étienne et compagnie ont fait leurs paiements en or."
"Oh! oh!" s'écria le drapier, "il faut être bien malade pour laisser voir sa bile. **Parlons d'autre chose**. Joseph, l'inventaire est fini."
"Oui, monsieur, et **le dividende est un des plus beaux que vous ayez eus**."
"Ne vous servez donc pas de ces nouveaux mots! Dites le produit, Joseph. Savez-vous, mon garçon, que c'est un peu à vous que nous devons ces résultats? Aussi, **ne veux-je plus que vous ayez d'appointements**. Madame Guillaume m'a donné l'idée de vous offrir un intérêt. Hein, Joseph! Guillaume et Lebas, ces mots ne feraient-ils pas une belle raison sociale? On pourrait mettre 'et compagnie' pour arrondir la signature."

1 If you didn't know the meaning of the verbs in the expressions "*asseyez-vous*" or "*Ne vous servez donc pas de . . .* ," how would you go about looking them up? (***Hint***: Knowing they're in the imperative is important.)
2 What is the relationship between the two men in the dialogue? What do you think is the purpose of Guillaume asking these questions?
3 What does Guillaume suggest at the end? Why do you think he does that?

4 Translate the highlighted phrases, and check your answers in the back of the book.

12 Present participles, past participles, and infinitives

I. Funny French!

To start: Find the one conjugated verb, the three unconjugated verbs, and the two adjectives. Look them up if you need to, and see if you can translate the joke.

MON INCROYABLE TALENT EST DE POUVOIR ÊTRE FATIGUÉE SANS RIEN FAIRE

Verify: Check your translation in the back of the book, and compare it to what you came up with. In this chapter we'll talk about how to translate unconjugated (infinitive) verbs, since they are treated differently in French and English. We'll also look at past participles that are used as adjectives, like the word *fatiguée* in this joke.

II. Vocabulary

In your reading, you will come across a wide variety of verbs used as present participles, past participles, or infinitives. To be prepared for that, let's take a look at a list of common French action verbs, divided by group. A few of these will be verbs you were already introduced to in Chapter 2, but I've included a good number of new action verbs as well, since these are likely to be used in the contexts we'll discuss in this chapter.

-*er* verbs

accepter	to accept	*jouer*	to play
attraper	to catch	*montrer*	to show
crier	to yell	*rester*	to stay
écouter	to listen to	*rêver*	to dream
enlever	to remove	*travailler*	to work
étudier	to study	*trouver*	to find
gagner	to win	*utiliser*	to use

-*ir* verbs

abolir	to abolish	*obéir*	to obey
agir	to act	*ouvrir*	to open
avertir[1]	to warn	*punir*	to punish
choisir	to choose	*réfléchir*	to reflect/think
établir	to establish	*réussir*	to succeed
finir	to finish	*saisir*	to seize/grab
grandir	to grow up	*tenir*	to hold

-*re* verbs

attendre	to wait for	*mordre*	to bite
défendre	to defend	*perdre*	to lose
dépendre	to depend on	*prétendre*	to claim
entendre	to hear	*répondre*	to respond
mettre	to put	*vendre*	to sell

Work with it

A. Which verbs from above are being described in the brief definitions below?

1. donner une peine pour un mauvais comportement ________
2. ne pas quitter l'endroit où l'on est ________
3. percevoir un son ________
4. interdire aux gens de faire quelque chose ________
5. échanger un bien pour de l'argent ________
6. parler très fort ________

B. Use what you've learned thus far to translate the phrases below, being sure to pay attention to the tense and mood.

Ex: nous rêvions   we were dreaming/we used to dream/we dreamed

1. il établira ________
2. vous avez attrapé ________
3. nous réussissons ________
4. elle a répondu ________
5. j'avertirais ________
6. elles entendront ________
7. tu choisissais ________
8. je trouve ________
9. vous vendrez ________

III. Grammar

A. *Present participles*

Present participles and gerunds (*-ing* verbs that function as nouns) present a unique problem for English speakers learning French, because in English we love to use the present progressive (e.g. "I am doing, he is going" instead of "I do, he goes"). French does not use this construction, so we must decide each time how to translate the simple present into English according to the context.

Elle chante. She sings./She is singing.
Nous regardons un film. We watch a film./We are watching a film.
Je te vois. I see you./I am seeing you.

This is not to say that the present participle isn't used in French; it just isn't used for the present progressive. Instead, you will see it used as a verb or gerund, and as a noun or adjective.

Formation: Just as the English present participle can be recognized by the ending *-ing*, the French present participle can be recognized by the ending *-ant*. This ending is added to a stem created by removing the present tense ending from the *nous* form of the verb.

	-*er* verbs	**-*ir* verbs**	**-*re* verbs**
Infinitive	parler	finir	attendre
Present tense	nous parl*ons*	nous finiss*ons*	nous attend*ons*
Present participle	parl*ant*	finiss*ant*	attend*ant*

There are three exceptions to the above formation. Two of these, *avoir* and *être*, are verbs that have irregular *nous* forms and therefore don't have the *-ons* ending to drop in the first place. The last one is *savoir*, whose typical present participle form has already been adopted as a word in its own right (*savant* = scholar). To avoid confusion, the subjunctive form is taken as the stem instead, with the usual *-ant* ending attached.

avoir → *ayant*
être → *étant*
savoir → *sachant*

Use: Let's start by looking at the French present participle as a verb and a gerund. We'll start with a few examples of each, and then I'll explain the difference.

Ayant *froid, j'ai décidé de porter un pull.*
Being cold, I decided to wear a sweater.

Je l'ai vu ***achetant*** *du pain pour notre dîner.*
I saw him **buying** bread for our dinner.
Regardant *son portable, elle n'a pas vu le bus.*
Looking at her phone, she didn't see the bus.

In these first three sentences, the present participle is used to modify a noun, giving additional information about the person mentioned.

Il aime regarder la télé ***en faisant*** *ses devoirs.*
He likes to watch TV **while doing** his homework.
En voyant *sa mère, elle s'est mise à pleurer.*
Upon seeing her mother, she began to cry.
Je ne peux pas écrire ***en entendant*** *du bruit.*
I can't write **while hearing** noise.

In these last three sentences, on the other hand, the present participle is used, along with the word *en*, to modify a verb. This is done to highlight the fact that both verbs are occurring at the same time ("while verb-ing") or that one verb caused the other ("upon verb-ing"). This is what the French refer to as *le gérondif*, or the gerund.

This distinction can be quite subtle at times. Remember to look out for that small word, *en*, to help you recognize the gerund form. It can mean the difference between seeing someone else doing an action and doing it oneself. For instance, watch what happens when I add the word *en* to one of the sentences above:

Je l'ai vu ***achetant*** *du pain.*	*Je l'ai vu* ***en achetant*** *du pain.*
I saw him **buying** bread.	I saw him **while buying** bread.

In the first case, the man I saw was buying bread, while in the second case I saw him while I was buying bread. This distinction can make a big difference in your understanding of a text.

Note: While these situations are translated with the gerund in English, there are cases where it is not an appropriate translation. For example, as we will see in section C, the present participle never comes after a conjugated verb, nor is it used to make a verb into a noun. These situations will require the infinitive form in French.

Present participles are also sometimes used as adjectives and nouns, so don't let the *-ant* fool you in words like:

Adjectives		Nouns	
amusant	amusing	*enseignant*	teacher
énervant	annoying	*gérant*	manager
intéressant	interesting	*participant*	participant

As a final note, although the present progressive is not used the same way in French and English, there is nevertheless a way to emphasize that someone is currently in the process of doing something. This is the expression *en train de,* which is used with the conjugated verb *être* and the action verb in its infinitive form.

Elle est ***en train de faire*** *ses devoirs.* — She's **doing** her homework.
Je suis ***en train de lui raconter*** *l'histoire.* — I'm **telling him** the story.
Nous sommes ***en train de décorer*** *la maison.* — We're **decorating** the house.

Work with it

A. Can you fill in the missing steps in the table showing how to form the present participle in French?

Infinitive →	*Nous* form, present tense →	Present participle
aller	*allons*	
rendre		*rendant*
choisir		*choisissant*
	écoutons	*écoutant*
faire	*faisons*	

B. Since most of the verbs in the contexts above will be translated with an *-ing* verb in English, the difficult part is not the translation itself. Rather, it's recognizing which French forms will become *-ing*, since there are several. In this exercise, underline the present participle in the English sentence as well as the corresponding word(s) in the French sentence.

1.	Tonight they're going to go dancing.	Ce soir elles vont aller danser.
2.	He likes walking while listening to music.	Il aime marcher en écoutant de la musique.
3.	I'm doing my homework right now.	Je fais mes devoirs en ce moment.
4.	Upon seeing his friend, he crosses the street.	En voyant son ami, il traverse la rue.
5.	She saw me doing my grocery shopping.	Elle m'a vue faisant les courses.
6.	You're in the process of moving, right?	Tu es en train de déménager, n'est-ce pas?

B. Past participles as adjectives

Just as in English, past participles can be used as adjectives in French. Here's a reminder of what the past participles look like in the different verb categories:

- the past participle of most *-er* verbs will end in *-é*
- the past participle of most *-ir* verbs will end in *i*
- the past participle of most *-re* verbs will end in *-u*

-*er* verbs		**-*ir* verbs**		**-*re* verbs**	
Infinitive	**Past participle**	**Infinitive**	**Past participle**	**Infinitive**	**Past participle**
parler	*parlé*	*finir*	*fini*	*attendre*	*attendu*
donner	*donné*	*choisir*	*choisi*	*rendre*	*rendu*
chanter	*chanté*	*partir*	*parti*	*entendre*	*entendu*

You may remember from Chapter 2 that in the compound past the past participle makes agreement with the subject only when *être* is its auxiliary. That is **not** the case here. Since these past participles are being used as adjectives, they are treated as such. This means they must make agreement with their noun in both gender and number, regardless of tense or verb.

Elle est bien ***connue*** *pour sa beauté.*	She is well **known** for her beauty.
Nous sommes ***énervés*** *aujourd'hui.*	We are **annoyed** today.
Je suis ***abasourdie*** *par son comportement.*	I am **flabbergasted** by her behavior.
Il est tout à fait ***dérouté*** *par le problème.*	He is completely **mystified** by the problem.
Elles semblent ***perdues*** *maintenant.*	They seem **lost** now.
Tu te trouves vraiment ***charmée*** *par lui?*	You really find yourself **charmed** by him?

The reason this can be difficult while reading in French is that you may be tempted to interpret these as past tense constructions, especially since you'll frequently see the verb *être* used with them. It's important to look at the context of the sentence to determine whether you're dealing with a verbal construction or a past participle used as an adjective.

Work with it

In the following list of adjectives (all in their masculine form), circle the ones you think come from past participles.

amical	joli	léger
rafraîchi	fâché	effrayé
gâté	cher	pensif
vieux	détendu	calme
gentil	passé	fatigué

C. Infinitive constructions

Infinitives can be found in many places in French: after a conjugated verb, following the prepositions *à* and *de*, when a verb is used as a noun, and in the past infinitive.

The most common place you'll find an infinitive is after a conjugated verb, as in the *futur proche* or with the verbs *vouloir, pouvoir, devoir,* and other verbs of preference. This is generally translated by the same construction in English:

*Je **veux aller** au cinéma demain.*	I **want to go** to the movies tomorrow.
*Nous **pouvons** vous **aider** à le faire.*	We **can help** you do it.
*Il **va arriver** chez nous bientôt.*	He's **going to arrive** at our house soon.
*Elles **préfèrent sortir** tous les soirs.*	They **prefer to go out** every night.

The infinitive also follows the prepositions *à* and *de* in various situations. In these cases, the preposition is not translated in English; rather, we use the infinitive alone.

*Il est difficile **de comprendre** ce texte.*	It's difficult **to understand** this text.
*Je suis triste **de voir** mon ex.*	I'm sad **to see** my ex.
*Nous avons demandé **de** le **voir**.*	We asked **to see** it.
*Elle apprend **à faire** des recherches.*	She's learning **to do** research.
*Je me suis mis **à chanter**.*	I started **to sing**.

A construction that involves both the infinitive and the past participle is called the past infinitive, and it is the equivalent of "having verb-ed." This structure uses the auxiliary verbs *avoir* or *être*, agreement is made as usual, and pronouns can be added. You may see it after the main clause of a sentence or with the preposition *après* (after).

*Il est content de m'**avoir rencontrée**.*	He is happy **to have met** me.
*Après **être partie**, elle a pleuré.*	After **having left**, she cried.
*Je suis ravi d'**avoir parlé** à ma mère.*	I'm thrilled **to have spoken** to my mother.
*Elles ont quitté le café après **avoir mangé**.*	They left the café after **having eaten**.

As you can see in the translations of these last four sentences, sometimes we use the infinitive in a similar way in English (as in the first and third sentences) and other times we use the present participle (as in the second and fourth sentences).

Finally, as I mentioned in the section on present participles, when using a verb as a noun (most often to refer to an activity in a general way), the infinitive is used in French (whereas the gerund is used in English).

J'aime ***danser****.*	I like to dance./I like **dancing**.
Lire *est mon passe-temps préféré.*	**Reading** is my favorite pastime.
Parler *n'est pas toujours facile.*	**Speaking** is not always easy.
Voir *c'est* ***croire****.*	**Seeing** is **believing**.

Negation: Negating an infinitive is different from negating a conjugated verb. In this case, the *ne . . . pas* stays together and is placed in front of the verb.

Elle préfère ***ne pas parler*** *de ce souvenir.*	She prefers **not to talk** about this memory.
Je suis soulagée de ***ne pas l'avoir vu****.*	I'm relieved **not to have seen** it.
Nous avons décidé de ***ne pas y aller****.*	We decided **not to go (there)**.

Work with it

A. Read the following short excerpt from *La culture des idées* by Remi de Gourmont (1900).

Écrire, c'est très différent de peindre ou de modeler; écrire ou parler, c'est user d'une faculté nécessairement commune à tous les hommes, d'une faculté primordiale et inconsciente. On ne peut l'analyser sans faire toute l'anatomie de l'intelligence; c'est pourquoi, qu'ils aient dix ou dix mille pages, tous les traités de l'art d'écrire sont de vaines esquisses. La question est si complexe qu'on ne sait par où l'aborder; elle a tant de pointes et c'est un tel buisson de ronces et d'épines qu'au lieu de s'y jeter on en fait le tour; et c'est prudent.

1. Can you list all the infinitives you see used as nouns?

   ____

2. What is the main topic (i.e. activity) of the passage? What other things is it compared to?

   ____

3. Is this activity easy? How do you know?

   ____

B. Using what you learned earlier about infinitive verbs, carefully read the following sentences, identify the infinitive constructions, and translate them.

1. C'est vrai que s'excuser n'est pas facile pour lui.

____

2. Mes étudiants se préparent à passer leurs examens.

____

3. Elle a choisi de ne pas passer ses vacances avec sa famille.

____

4. Après s'être rendu compte du niveau de difficulté, elles ont abandonné le projet.

____

IV. Reading and translation

Read this short excerpt from *Prétextes: Réflexions sur quelques points de littérature et de morale* by André Gide (1919), and answer the questions below.

> Mais combien celui qui, sans avoir une personnalité fatale, toute d'ombre et d'éblouissement, **tâche de se créer une personnalité restreinte et combinée, en se privant de certaines influences**, en se mettant l'esprit au régime, comme un malade dont l'estomac débile ne saurait supporter qu'un choix de nourritures peu variées (mais qu'alors il digère si bien!) – **combien celui-là me fait aimer le dilettante, qui, ne pouvant être producteur et parler, prend le charmant parti d'être attentif** et se fait une carrière vraiment de savoir admirablement écouter.

1 This text has a good number of past participles as adjectives, present participles and gerunds, and infinitives. Can you find and translate them all?

2 This excerpt is 85 words, but only one sentence! This is done by linking several ideas together, many of which give extra information about the subject but don't advance the sentence. Can you figure out who or what is the subject of the sentence? (***Hint***: It's a demonstrative pronoun.)

3 What are the two verbs that refer directly to this subject? (***Hint***: One is in the second line and one is in the fifth line.)

4 Translate the highlighted portions and check your answers in the back of the book.

____

____

____

____

Note

1 This verb is the origin of the noun *avertissement,* which is a false friend. Though it looks like the English word "advertisement," it means "warning."

13 Simple past

I. Funny French!

To start: Rather than using a verb in the *passé simple*, this joke makes a pun about it. Can you figure it out?

A l'école,
on apprend le passé simple,
mais rien sur
le futur compliqué.

Verify: Check the translation in the back of the book. Were you right?

II. Vocabulary

In this chapter we're going to look at a strictly literary tense called the *passé simple*. This would be the direct translation of the simple past we use in English (with *-ed*) except that in French it evolved in such a way that it is no longer used in speech. It is now found only in writing, and as you do research or read literary works, you will encounter it often.

Speaking of literary language, French literature is also a place where you are likely to encounter vocabulary that is more elevated than that of everyday, spoken language. Here are just a few words you may see in academic and/or literary texts:

abasourdi	adj stunned
abnégation	n self-denial
affubler	v dress up in
ainsi	adv in this way/thus
apercevoir	v to catch sight of
bafouer	v to flout/ridicule
contrée	n region/land
craindre	v to fear
ébaudir	v to entertain
ébouriffant	adj breathtaking
efflanqué	adj emaciated
entamer	v to start on
épanoui	adj glowing/radiant
errant	adj wandering/nomadic
fuir	v to flee
gémir	v to whine/moan
hautain	adj haughty
munir	v to equip
paraître	v to seem/to appear
peiner	v to struggle
valoir	v to be worth

Work with it

In the following sentences, choose one of the elevated vocabulary items from the list above to replace the highlighted word.

1. Elle s'inquiétait pour le cheval **maigre** qu'elle avait vu dans l'écurie. ______________
2. Il préfère de loin **s'habiller bien** quand il part à une soirée. ________
3. Soudain ils **ont vu** l'homme mystérieux qu'ils cherchaient. _______
4. La pièce de théâtre va **divertir** tous les spectateurs. ____________
5. Il faut **équiper** les alpinistes de cordes pour la montée. ___________

III. Grammar

The *passé simple* is fairly recognizable by its endings, but those endings are not the same for all verbs, and there are several irregular verbs. Let's take a look at the formation of the *passé simple* before moving on to its use.

Formation: For this tense we'll need to look at the verb groups separately, since the *-er* verbs take a different ending than the *-ir* and *-re* verbs. Here are the *passé simple* endings for the different verb groups:

-*er* verbs				**-*ir* and -*re* verbs**			
je	*-ai*	*nous*	*-âmes*	*je*	*-is*	*nous*	*-îmes*
tu	*-as*	*vous*	*-âtes*	*tu*	*-is*	*vous*	*-îtes*
il/elle/on	*-a*	*ils/elles*	*-èrent*	*il/elle/on*	*-it*	*ils/elles*	*-irent*

These endings are added to a stem consisting of the infinitive minus *-er*, *-ir*, or *-re*.

Here are three sentences from *La marquise de Sade* by Rachilde (1888) showing examples of regular verbs from each verb group:

> Mary **s'arrêta** prise de colère.
>
> "Non, je ne veux plus!" **répéta**-t-elle en enfonçant ses ongles dans le poignet de la cousine.
>
> Elles **sortirent** de l'abattoir sans se parler. Chose singulière, Mary n'avait pas versé une larme.
>
> . . . elle **entendit** la voix du colonel dire sur un ton de colère . . .

There are three common irregular verbs to know in the *passé simple*, and you will see them often. Like the regular verbs listed above, they'll be recognizable by their endings, particularly the *accent circonflexe* (*â, î, û*). As usual, these irregular verbs are *avoir*, *être*, and *faire*.

avoir	*être*	*faire*
j'eus	*je fus*	*je fis*
tu eus	*tu fus*	*tu fis*
il eut	*elle fut*	*on fit*
nous eûmes	*nous fûmes*	*nous fîmes*
vous eûtes	*vous fûtes*	*vous fîtes*
ils eurent	*elles furent*	*ils firent*

You may see the word *faire* used in the *passé simple* to introduce dialogue. Consider the following examples, again from *La marquise de Sade* by Rachilde:

> "Encore ça! . . ." **fit**-elle avec désespoir; "tu es une sotte, il n'y a pas de lait ici et tu n'en boiras pas."
>
> "La voilà qui me griffe, à présent!" **fit**-elle . . .

Just by knowing the *passé simple* verb endings, you'll be able to recognize them fairly well while reading. It's not necessary to know all the irregular verb stems, but here are just a few of the most common remaining irregular forms. You might notice that, with the exception of *tenir*, the *passé simple* form is based on the past participle:

devoir	***pouvoir***	***prendre***	***tenir***	***vivre***
je dus	*je pus*	*je pris*	*je tins*	*je vécus*
tu dus	*tu pus*	*tu pris*	*tu tins*	*tu vécus*
il dus	*elle put*	*on prit*	*il tint*	*elle vécut*
nous dûmes	*nous pûmes*	*nous prîmes*	*nous tînmes*	*nous vécûmes*
vous dûtes	*vous pûtes*	*vous prîtes*	*vous tîntes*	*vous vécûtes*
ils durent	*elles purent*	*ils prirent*	*elles tinrent*	*ils vécurent*

Use: The *passé simple* is used in the same way as the *passé composé*, and relates to the *imparfait* in the same way as well. Consider the following short excerpt from *Notre-dame de Paris* by Victor Hugo (1831), and compare the way the *passé simple* (bold) is used in relation to the other tenses (italicized).

> *C'était* en effet le recteur et tous les dignitaires de l'Université qui *se rendaient* processionnellement au-devant de l'ambassade et *traversaient* en ce moment la place du Palais. Les écoliers, pressés à la fenêtre, les **accueillirent** au passage avec des sarcasmes et des applaudissements ironiques. Le recteur, qui *marchait* en tête de sa compagnie, **essuya** la première bordée; elle **fut** rude.

Notice that narration is done the same way here as it was in Chapter 5 where we looked at the imperfect and the *passé composé*. The italicized words above describe either states of being or actions that were continuous or habitual in the past. The words in the *passé simple*, on the other hand, describe completed actions:

Les écoliers . . . les ***accueillirent*** *au passage*	The schoolchildren greeted them in passing
Le recteur . . . ***essuya*** *la première bordée*	The rector . . . endured the first volley
. . . elle ***fut*** *rude*	. . . it was formidable

Work with it

A. Scan the following dialogue from *Inutile beauté* by Guy de Maupassant (1890) and find all the examples of the *passé simple*. Sort them into the table below based on their category: *-er* verbs, *-ir* and *-re* verbs, or *avoir/être/faire*. Don't worry about repetitions, just list each verb once.

À la fin, il glissa sournoisement sa main vers la main gantée de la comtesse et la toucha comme par hasard, mais le geste qu'elle fit en retirant son bras fut si vif et si plein de dégoût qu'il demeura anxieux, malgré ses habitudes d'autorité et de despotisme.

Alors il murmura:

"Gabrielle!"

Elle demanda, sans tourner la tête:

"Que voulez-vous?"

"Je vous trouve adorable."

Elle ne répondit rien, et demeurait étendue dans sa voiture avec un air de reine irritée.

. . .

Le comte de Mascaret reprit:

"Ma chère Gabrielle."

Alors, n'y tenant plus, elle répliqua d'une voix exaspérée:

"Oh! laissez-moi tranquille, je vous prie. Je n'ai même plus la liberté d'être seule dans ma voiture, à présent."

Il simula n'avoir point écouté, et continua:

"Vous n'avez jamais été aussi jolie qu'aujourd'hui."

Elle était certainement à bout de patience et elle répliqua avec une colère qui ne se contenait point:

"Vous avez tort de vous en apercevoir, car je vous jure bien que je ne serai plus jamais à vous."

Certes, il fut stupéfait et bouleversé, et, ses habitudes de violence reprenant le dessus, il jeta un – "Qu'est-ce à dire?" qui révélait plus le maître brutal que l'homme amoureux.

***-er* verbs (9)**		***-ir/-re* verbs (2)**	***avoir/être/faire* (2)**

B. In the following short excerpt from *Un coeur simple* by Gustave Flaubert (1877), underline the verbs in imperfect and circle the verbs in *passé simple*. Then look at the two words or expressions I've listed below and describe what they are.

Et du bras gauche il lui entoura la taille; elle marchait soutenue par son étreinte; ils se ralentirent. Le vent était mou, les étoiles brillaient, l'énorme charretée de foin oscillait devant eux; et les quatre chevaux, en traînant leurs pas, soulevaient de la poussière. Puis, sans commandement, ils tournèrent à droite. Il l'embrassa encore une fois. Elle disparut dans l'ombre.

1. soutenue ____

2. en traînant ______________________________________

C. Now translate the following selected sentences from the two previous exercises.

1. Elle ne répondit rien, et demeurait étendue dans sa voiture avec un air de reine irritée.

____

2. Puis, sans commandement, ils tournèrent à droite.

____

3. Il l'embrassa encore une fois. Elle disparut dans l'ombre.

____

IV. Reading and translation

Read the following excerpt from *L'inutile beauté* by Guy de Maupassant (1890), and answer the questions below.

La comtesse de Mascaret se montra sur le perron juste au moment où son mari, qui rentrait, arriva sous la porte cochère. Il s'arrêta quelques secondes pour regarder sa femme, et il pâlit un peu. Elle était fort belle, svelte, distinguée avec sa longue figure ovale, son teint d'ivoire doré, ses grands yeux gris et ses cheveux noirs; et **elle monta dans sa voiture sans le regarder, sans paraître même l'avoir aperçu**, avec une allure si particulièrement racée, que l'infâme jalousie dont il était depuis si longtemps dévoré, le mordit au coeur de nouveau. Il s'approcha, et la saluant:

"Vous allez vous promener?" dit-il.

Elle laissa passer quatre mots entre ses lèvres dédaigneuses.

"Vous le voyez bien!"
"Au bois?"
"C'est probable."
"Me serait-il permis de vous accompagner?"
"La voiture est à vous."

Sans s'étonner du ton dont elle lui répondait, il monta et s'assit a côté de sa femme, puis il ordonna:

"Au bois."

1 After reading a first time, take time to identify all the verbs. Which ones are in imperfect and which are in *passé simple*? Of those in *passé simple*, do you see verbs from all categories?

2 What is the nature of the relationship between the countess and her husband? What gives you this impression?

3 There's one verb in the conditional. What's going on with that sentence?

4 Translate the phrases in bold, and check your answers in the back of the book.

14 More compound tenses

I. Funny French!

To start: It will help you to know that *un truc* is slang for "a thing." Now find the two conjugated verbs and look at the difference between them. With the tenses you've learned so far, can you figure out the translation of the expression *j'aurai fini*?

J'irai chercher un truc à manger
quand j'aurai fini le prochain
niveau de Candy Crush

Verify: Look up any words you're unsure of, and check your translation in the back of the book.

II. Vocabulary

Let's review some of the vocabulary we've seen up to this point. In Chapter 5 we learned the following adverbs and expressions of time that deal with past events:

actuellement	currently	*après*	after
aujourd'hui	today	*auparavant*	previously, beforehand
avant	before	*bientôt*	soon
d'abord	first	*déjà*	already
enfin	finally	*ensuite*	next
hier	yesterday	*maintenant*	now
récemment	recently	*souvent*	often
tout à coup	suddenly	*toujours*	always

In Chapter 10 we looked at the following expressions of time that are typically used to refer to future events:

après-demain	the day after tomorrow
aussitôt	as soon as
bientôt	soon
demain	tomorrow
dès que	as soon as
dorénavant	from now on
lorsque	when
quand	when

In the compound tenses we'll see in this chapter we may need more expressions of time, so let's look at a few of those:

à l'avenir	in the future
à la fois	at the same time
à temps	on time
alors	then
au fil du temps	over time

au fur et à mesure	as, gradually
autrefois	in the past
désormais	from now on
en même temps	at the same time
il y a	ago
jadis	once, in olden days
longtemps	(for a) long time
précédemment	previously
tout à l'heure	a little while ago/in a little while

Work with it

A. Which of these new expressions of time is most logical in the following sentences? Pay attention to the tenses for clues.

1. ______________________, c'était le gouvernement qui s'en occupait.

2. Le prof a confirmé que ________________, des interrogations seront requises.

3. Elle a conclu que ce ne serait pas possible de faire ces deux choses ________________.

4. Ma fille m'a dit qu' ________________ elle deviendra astronaute.

5. Mon mari a décidé d'obtenir son doctorat il y a très ________.

B. Do the answers in the back of the book match your own? If not, can you see why not? In order to understand these expressions a little better, try to translate the following sentences.

1. Au fur et à mesure que le chômage monte, la situation devient précaire.

____.

2. Je viens de la voir dans le couloir tout à l'heure.

____.

3. Jadis un bel endroit prospère, il est maintenant désert.

____.

III. Grammar

A. Pluperfect and le passé antérieur

The pluperfect and the *passé antérieur* are two structures that express the same idea, which is that one event happened further in the past than another event. We'll look at the difference in structure later, but first let's look at a few examples of the pluperfect with English translations to help clarify the meaning.

> *Quand ils sont arrivés, **elle était** déjà **partie**.*
> When they arrived, **she had** already **left**.
> *J'ai remarqué **qu'il avait mangé** le pain.*
> I noticed that **he had eaten** the bread.
> ***Tu avais** déjà **appris** la leçon quand nous y avons travaillé ensemble en classe.*
> **You had learned** the lesson when we worked on it together in class.

Notice that the previous action, expressed by the pluperfect, can be mentioned in the first or second part of the sentence. You may also see the word *déjà* (already) used with this construction, placed between the auxiliary verb and the past participle. The more recent action in the sentence is in the *passé composé.*

Formation: As compound tenses, both the pluperfect and the *passé antérieur* are formed using an auxiliary verb and a past participle. As always, *avoir* and *être* are used, and *être* verbs make agreement in gender and number with their subject. The difference between the two is that in the pluperfect, the auxiliary verb is conjugated in the imperfect, while in the *passé antérieur* it's conjugated in the simple past. Consider the following table, which shows the verbs *donner* (to give) and *aller* (to go) in each construction:

	Pluperfect	***Passé antérieur***	**Pluperfect**	***Passé antérieur***
je	*avais donné*	*eus donné*	*étais allé(e)*	*fus allé(e)*
tu	*avais donné*	*eus donné*	*étais allé(e)*	*fus allé(e)*
il/elle/on	*avait donné*	*eut donné*	*était allé(e)*	*fut allé(e)*
nous	*avions donné*	*eûmes donné*	*étions allé(e)s*	*fûmes allé(e)s*

	Pluperfect	*Passé antérieur*	Pluperfect	*Passé antérieur*
vous	*aviez donné*	*eûtes donné*	*étiez allé(e)s*	*fûtes allé(e)(s)*
ils/elles	*avaient donné*	*eurent donné*	*étaient allé(e)s*	*furent allé(e)s*

Use: The pluperfect is usually used alongside the *passé composé*, and the *passé antérieur* goes along with the simple past, though you will surely see a mixture of all of them in some texts. Consider the following two examples from *Micromégas* by Voltaire (1752):

Après que **son excellence se fut couchée**, et que **le secrétaire se fut approché** de son visage, Il faut avouer, dit Micromégas, que la nature est bien variée.

Quand **ils eurent fait** environ cent cinquante millions de lieues, ils rencontrèrent les satellites de Jupiter.

Note: You might have noticed that the examples of *passé antérieur* in the first sentence are reflexive verbs: *se coucher* and *s'approcher de*. These are treated the same way here as they are in the *passé composé*: that is, the reflexive pronoun comes before the auxiliary verb.

Now compare the examples above to the following excerpt from *Les plaisirs et les jours* by Marcel Proust (1896):

Certes, depuis le jour où **il avait entendu dire** que la maladie de son oncle était inguérissable, **Alexis l'avait vu** plusieurs fois. Mais depuis, **tout avait bien changé**. **Baldassare s'était rendu compte** de son mal et savait maintenant qu'il avait au plus trois ans à vivre. Alexis, sans comprendre d'ailleurs comment **cette certitude n'avait pas tué de chagrin ou rendu fou** son oncle, se sentait incapable de supporter la douleur de le voir.

Work with it

Let's use the excerpts above to work with the pluperfect and the *passé antérieur*. Using the verb conjugation chart below (the *passé simple*), transform the pluperfect into the *passé antérieur* by replacing the auxiliary verb. I've done the first as a model.

avoir		être	
j'eus	*nous eûmes*	*je fus*	*nous fûmes*
tu eus	*vous eûtes*	*tu fus*	*vous fûtes*
il/elle/on eut	*ils/elles eurent*	*il/elle/on fut*	*ils/elles furent*

Ex: il avait entendu dire   il eut entendu dire

1. nous l'avions vu ______________________
2. tout avait bien changé ______________________
3. ils s'étaient rendu compte ______________________
4. elle n'avait pas tué son oncle ______________________
5. je n'avais pas rendu le livre ______________________

B. Future perfect

You saw the future perfect in the joke at the beginning of this chapter (*j'aurai fini* = I will have finished). It's used to refer to events, actions, or states that will be accomplished in the future – in other words, it's the past in the future. Much like the future tense, we might not always translate the French future perfect into the English future perfect, even though we have that tense/aspect combination.

*D'ici la fin de l'année, **j'aurai terminé** mes études.*
By the end of the year, **I will have finished** my studies.
***Ils seront arrivés** à la gare avant 18h00.*
They will have arrived at the train station before 6:00 p.m.
*Quand tu arriveras **elle aura fait** le ménage.*
When you arrive **she will have done** the housework.
*J'irai chercher un truc à manger quand **j'aurai fini** le prochain niveau de Candy Crush.*
I'll go find something to eat when **I've finished/I finish** the next level of Candy Crush.

Notice that in the last sentence, the one from this chapter's joke, I didn't use the future perfect in my translation. While future perfect is used in French in this case, because it's referring to an action that *will be completed* in the future, it sounds awkward to use it in English.

Formation: Continuing with the theme of compound tenses, the future perfect uses *avoir* or *être* as an auxiliary verb – this time conjugated in the simple future – along with the past participle of the action verb. As always, the past participle of verbs that take *être* as their auxiliary makes agreement in both gender and number with the subject of the sentence. Regardless of auxiliary verb, they are translated as "will have" in English (if they're translated using the future perfect at all).

	***avoir* verbs**		***être* verbs**	
	Future	**Past participle**	**Future**	**Past participle**
je	*aurai*	*fini*	*serai*	*venu(e)*
tu	*auras*	*fini*	*seras*	*venu(e)*
il/elle/on	*aura*	*fini*	*sera*	*venu(e)*
nous	*aurons*	*fini*	*serons*	*venu(e)s*
vous	*aurez*	*fini*	*serez*	*venu(e)(s)*
ils/elles	*auront*	*fini*	*seront*	*venu(e)s*

As with other compound tenses, negation goes around the auxiliary verb. Check out the following sentences and reflect on the position of the negation and why there is or isn't agreement made on the past participle:

> *Dans un mois, **nous n'aurons pas déménagé** à Paris.*
> In one month, **we will not have moved** to Paris.
> ***Elles ne seront pas** encore **parties** quand vous arriverez.*
> **They will not have left** yet when you arrive.
> *Je ne te verrai pas si **tu n'auras pas fini** tes devoirs.*
> I'll not see you if **you haven't finished** your homework.

Notice that although the future perfect is used in all three sentences in French, it isn't always translated that way in English. While the first two sentences are translated in future perfect, the third is translated using the present perfect.

If pronouns are involved, whether direct, indirect, or reflexive, they go in their usual place, before the conjugated verb:

Les enfants se seront couchés *quand leur père rentrera.*
The kids will have gone to bed when their father gets back.
Je lui en aurai parlé *avant la fête ce weekend.*
I will have talked to him about it before the party this weekend.
Il sera heureux dès que ***nous l'aurons vue****.*
He will be happy as soon as **we've seen her**.

Use: The future perfect is used not only to refer to events, actions, or states that will be completed in the future, but also to speculate about things that might have happened and to refer to historical events. For example, you may see sentences like the following:

Marie n'était pas en classe aujourd'hui; ***elle sera*** *sûrement* ***tombée*** *malade.*
Marie wasn't in class today; **she must have gotten** sick.
Charles Baudelaire aura publié Les Fleurs du Mal *en 1857.*
Charles Baudelaire published *Les Fleurs de Mal* in 1857.

Work with it

A. For the following sentences, find the future perfect and decide how it is being used: to talk about future completed actions (CA), to speculate (SP), or as part of a historical narrative (HN).

1. Il ne trouve pas sa montre; il l'aura laissée chez son ami. ________
2. Nous aurons fait les croissants quand tu te lèveras. ________
3. Mes parents nous rendront visite une fois qu'on aura acheté un lit. ________
4. Le roi aura assassiné ses ennemis lors du bal. ________
5. Tu as l'air malade; tu auras attrapé un rhume. ________

B. Now think carefully about whether each of the sentences above would be translated by the future perfect in English or by some other tense/aspect combination.

1. ____
2. ____

3. ____
4. ____
5. ____

C. Conditional perfect

The conditional perfect is much like the future perfect, except that it describes events, actions, or states that will be hypothetically completed in the future. It's the equivalent of English "would have + past participle."

Formation: The conditional perfect looks very similar to the future perfect. Change the auxiliary verb from future to conditional and you're done! When reading, then, it will be important to recognize the endings that signal conditional over future. Remember that they have the same stem, but the ending is slightly different. This means that for most of the subject pronouns, you'll see an *-i-* that wasn't there before (e.g. *tu auras* → *tu aurais*). For the subject *je*, the only difference is the addition of an *-s-* (*j'aurai* → *j'aurais*).

	***avoir* verbs**		***être* verbs**	
	Conditional	**Past participle**	**Conditional**	**Past participle**
je	*aurais*	*fini*	*serais*	*venu(e)*
tu	*aurais*	*fini*	*serais*	*venu(e)*
il/elle/on	*aurait*	*fini*	*serait*	*venu(e)*
nous	*aurions*	*fini*	*serions*	*venu(e)s*
vous	*auriez*	*fini*	*seriez*	*venu(e)(s)*
ils/elles	*auraient*	*fini*	*seraient*	*venu(e)s*

Use: As you might imagine, the conditional perfect injects a lack of certainty into the event, action, or state described. You'll notice that it is frequently used alongside the pluperfect, especially in "if . . . then" statements. For example:

S'il avait mangé le déjeuner ***il n'aurait pas eu*** *faim.*
If he had eaten lunch **he wouldn't have been** hungry.

Nous serions venus *si nous avions su que c'était important.*
We would have come if we had known it was important.
Elles auraient réussi *si elles avaient fait un effort.*
They would have succeeded if they had made an effort.

Work with it

A. To work on distinguishing between future and conditional perfect, match the verb phrase on the left with its appropriate translation on the right.

1.	nous serions allés	**a.**	he would have done
2.	il aura fait	**b.**	they will have sold
3.	elles auraient vendu	**c.**	we will have gone
4.	elles auront vendu	**d.**	we would have gone
5.	il aurait fait	**e.**	he will have done
6.	nous serons allés	**f.**	they would have sold

B. Look closely at the verbs below to match the *si* clauses on the left to their corresponding conditional clause on the right (***Hint***: There will be imperfect/conditional sets as well as pluperfect/conditional perfect sets).

1.	S'il avait fait attention . . .	**a.**	. . . vous auriez été surpris.
2.	Si nous allions au marché . . .	**b.**	. . . nous aurions gagné moins d'argent.
3.	Si vous aviez vu la taille de sa voiture . . .	**c.**	. . . il n'aurait pas eu un accident.
4.	S'il était venu avec nous . . .	**d.**	. . . il aurait apprécié notre blague.
5.	Si nous étions devenus profs . . .	**e.**	. . . vous m'appelleriez.
6.	Si vous vouliez me parler . . .	**f.**	. . . nous achèterions des pommes.

D. Past subjunctive

There are three versions of the subjunctive, above and beyond the present subjunctive that we saw in Chapter 11. Here we'll concentrate mostly on the past subjunctive, but I will also show you the imperfect and pluperfect forms so you can recognize them in texts.

Use: Much of the time, the subjunctive clause of the sentence can stay in the present tense even when the introductory clause changes time frame.

Je veux que ***tu viennes*** *avec moi.*	I want **you to come** with me.
Je voulais que ***tu viennes*** *avec moi.*	I wanted **you to come** with me.
Je voudrais que ***tu viennes*** *avec moi.*	I would like **you to come** with me.

This is because there's an understanding that both things are happening or did happen at the same point in time. However, if the action (subjunctive clause) took place in the past and I'm describing how I feel about it at the present moment (introductory clause), I will use the past subjunctive.

Elle est ravie que ***tu sois venu.***	She's delighted that **you came**.
Il est triste que ***tu n'aies pas pu*** *le voir.*	It's sad that **you weren't able** to see it.
*Je doute qu'****ils aient fait*** *le ménage.*	I doubt that **they did** the housework.

Formation: As you can see, it is the auxiliary verb that changes to reflect the subjunctive mood. Either *avoir* or *être* is conjugated in the present tense form of the subjunctive, and the past participle of the action verb is used.

Pluperfect and imperfect subjunctive: Although they are less common, you may also come across pluperfect and imperfect versions of the subjunctive:

	Pluperfect		**Imperfect**	
	chanter	***venir***	***chanter***	***venir***
je	*eusse chanté*	*fusse venu(e)*	*chantasse*	*vinsse*
tu	*eusses chanté*	*fusses venu(e)*	*chantasses*	*vinsses*
il/elle/on	*eût chanté*	*fût venu(e)*	*chantât*	*vînt*
nous	*eussions chanté*	*fussions venu(e)s*	*chantassions*	*vinssions*

	Pluperfect		Imperfect	
	chanter	**venir**	**chanter**	**venir**
vous	*eussiez chanté*	*fussiez venu(e)(s)*	*chantassiez*	*vinssiez*
ils/elles	*eussent chanté*	*fussent venu(e)s*	*chantassent*	*vinssent*

Notice that the imperfect subjunctive is a simple tense, so there is only one word conjugated in this construction. Pluperfect subjunctive, on the other hand, is a compound tense – so you'll see an auxiliary verb in a distinctive form along with a past participle you already recognize.

But what do these past subjunctive constructions mean? How do we translate them? Let's take a look at an example of imperfect subjunctive from *L'inutile beauté* by Guy de Maupassant (1890):

> *Elle répéta, à voix basse, bien que* ***leurs gens ne pussent rien entendre*** *dans l'assourdissant ronflement des roues.*
>
> She repeated, in a low voice, although **their people could hear nothing** in the deafening roar of the wheels.

There are a couple of things happening in this sentence. First of all, we have the conjunction *bien que* ("even though" or "although"), which triggers the subjunctive. Secondly, all of the actions described are in the past tense. The sentence starts with *elle répéta,* which is the *passé simple* equivalent of the compound past *elle a répété,* so we know that the next part will refer to something that *was happening* in the past (imperfect subjunctive).

The pluperfect subjunctive is simply the literary equivalent of the past subjunctive. Instead of conjugating the auxiliary verb in the present subjunctive, it's conjugated in the imperfect subjunctive before adding the past participle. Consider the differences:

Il craignait qu'elle soit perdue. *Il craignait qu'elle fût perdue.*	He feared she was lost.
Je ne crois pas que tu aies réussi. *Je ne crois pas que tu eusses réussi.*	I don't believe that you succeeded.
Il est étonnant que nous l'ayons vu. *Il est étonnant que nous l'eussions vu.*	It's shocking that we saw it.

Work with it

A. This exercise doesn't require you to write anything down. Analyze the following sentence pairs, where one is in the present subjunctive and the other is in the past subjunctive. Can you understand what each sentence means, and see the difference denoted by the tense change?

1. Il est dommage que tu sois malade. / Il est dommage que tu aies été malade.
2. Elle est ravie que son père vienne. / Elle est ravie que son père soit venu.
3. Je doute qu'il fasse le ménage. / Je doute qu'il ait fait le ménage.
4. Elles ont peur que je ne mange pas. / Elles ont peur que je n'aie pas mangé.

B. Can you recognize the imperfect and the pluperfect subjunctive? Read the following sentences and circle IS or PS.

1. Elle les appela bien qu'ils eussent arrivés avant elle. IS/PS
2. Nous partîmes de peur qu'il ne fût pas prêt. IS/PS
3. Elle fut triste que tu chantasses cet hymne. IS/PS
4. Il est douteux que je l'eusse compris. IS/PS

IV. Reading and translation

Read this excerpt from *L'archipel en feu* by Jules Verne (1884) and answer the questions below.

"Une sacolève!" **s'écrièrent** ses compagnons, dont le désappointement **se traduisit** par une bordée de jurons. Mais, à ce sujet, il n'y **eut** aucune discussion, parce qu'il n'y avait pas d'erreur possible. Le navire, qui manoeuvrait à l'entrée du golfe de Coron, était bien une sacolève. Après tout, ces gens de Vitylo avaient tort de crier à la malchance. Il n'est pas rare de trouver quelque cargaison précieuse à bord de ces sacolèves.

On appelle ainsi un bâtiment levantin de médiocre tonnage, dont la tonture, c'est-à-dire la courbe du pont, s'accentue légèrement en se relevant vers l'arrière. . . . Rien de plus élégant que ce léger bâtiment, se couchant et se redressant à la lame, se couronnant d'écume, bondissant sans effort, semblable à quelque énorme oiseau, dont les ailes **eussent rasé** la mer, qui brasillait alors sous les derniers rayons du soleil.

Bien que la brise **tendît** à fraîchir et que le ciel **se couvrît** d'"échillons" – nom que les Levantins donnent à certains nuages de leur ciel – la sacolève ne diminuait rien de sa voilure. Elle avait même conservé son perroquet volant, qu'un marin moins audacieux **eût** certainement **amené**. Évidemment, c'était dans l'intention d'atterrir, le capitaine ne se souciant pas de passer la nuit sur une mer déjà dure et qui menaçait de grossir encore.

1 Looking at the words in bold, identify three examples of the *passé simple*, two examples of the imperfect subjunctive, and two examples of the pluperfect subjunctive.

2 A *sacolève* is a merchant sailing ship with three masts. How is it described in the second paragraph?

3 How did the narrator's companions react to seeing the *sacolève*? Were they right to react that way, according to him?

4 Try your hand at the imperfect and pluperfect subjunctive moods by translating the last paragraph. Check your answer in the back of the book.

15 Common academic and idiomatic constructions

I. Funny French!

To start: It's another cat meme! The word *vaut* is from the verb *valoir*, which means "to be worth." Knowing that, can you figure out the joke?

quand tu veux commencer un débat avec quelqu'un mais que tu réalises que ça n'en vaut pas la peine

Verify: Looking at the translation in the back of the book, you see that the expression ". . . ne vaut pas la peine de . . ." means that something is not worth (the pain of) taking a given action. In this chapter we'll look at more idiomatic and academic constructions that aren't necessarily obvious when translated literally.

II. Vocabulary

At this point you should feel fairly comfortable with the basic structures you'll come across while reading in French, but I would be remiss if I didn't also introduce to you some of the specialized vocabulary and grammar that mark academic writing.

A. Transition words

Transition and linking words are indispensable to understanding both individual sentences and how they relate to one another. These linking words are especially prevalent in academic writing and philosophy. Study this list and then complete the exercise below to see these transition words in action.

à cet effet	to this end
ainsi	in this way, thus
ainsi que	just as, as well as
alors que	while, whereas
autant que	as much as
autrement dit	in other words
bien que	even though
bref	in short
cependant	yet, even so
comme	just as, as well as
d'autant plus	especially as
de toute façon	anyway
donc	therefore, so
en fait	in fact
en outre	furthermore

en premier lieu	in the first place
en revanche	on the other hand
malgré	despite
néanmoins	nevertheless
par ailleurs	in addition, also
par contre	on the other hand
pourtant	however
puisque	since, as
quant à	as for
quoi que	whatever
sinon	otherwise, if not
soit . . . soit	. . . either . . . or . . .
tandis que	while, whereas

Work with it

A. Read the following excerpt from *Cours de philosophie positive* by Auguste Comte (1830), a famous French philosopher. Find and circle four of the transition words from the list above.

Ainsi, pour en citer l'exemple le plus admirable, nous disons que les phénomènes généraux de l'univers sont expliqués, autant qu'ils puissent l'être, par la loi de la gravitation newtonienne, parce que, d'un côté, cette belle théorie nous montre toute l'immense variété des faits astronomiques, comme n'étant qu'un seul et même fait envisagé sous divers points de vue; la tendance constante de toutes les molécules les unes vers les autres en raison directe de leurs masses, et en raison inverse des carrés de leurs distances; tandis que, d'un autre côté, ce fait général nous est présenté comme une simple extension d'un phénomène qui nous est éminemment familier, et que, par cela seul, nous regardons comme parfaitement connu, la pesanteur des corps à la surface de la terre. Quant à déterminer ce que sont en elles-mêmes cette attraction et cette pesanteur, quelles en sont les causes, ce sont des questions que nous regardons tous comme insolubles, qui ne sont plus du domaine de la philosophie positive, et que nous abandonnons avec raison à l'imagination des théologiens, ou aux subtilités des métaphysiciens.

B. Now turn to the back of the book and compare the listed words to those you found. Write them below, along with a brief translation of the phrase they're found in (you don't need to translate the whole sentence, just enough to show the use of the transition word).

1. ____________________ ____________________________________

2. ____________________ ____________________________________

3. ____________________ ____________________________________

4. ____________________ ____________________________________

B. Common academic vocabulary

To further understand academic texts, you should be familiar with some of the expressions that authors use to present opinions and make arguments. Here are just a few of the most common:

à mon avis	in my opinion
cela va sans dire que	it goes without saying that
considérons	let us consider
d'après moi	according to me
d'une part, d'autre part	on one hand, on the other hand
en ce qui concerne . . .	as far as . . . is concerned
il est question de	it's a matter of
il (me) semble que	it seems (to me) that
je constate que	I note that/I observe that
j'estime que	I consider that
je voudrais souligner que	I would like to underline that
quoi qu'il en soit	be that as it may
tout bien considéré	all things considered

Work with it

For each of the sentences below, choose the expression that makes the most sense in context as well as within the grammatical structure of the sentence:

1. [Considérons/J'estime] le fait qu'il n'existe que trois temps verbaux.
2. [Il est question de/Cela va sans dire que] le présent s'emploie le plus souvent.
3. [Il est question de/En ce qui concerne] les autres éléments, ils sont plus compliqués.
4. [Je constate que/Tout bien considéré] les étudiants le trouvent difficile à maîtriser.

C. *A few idiomatic expressions*

Idiomatic expressions are usually used in oral communication, but since dialogue can be a main component of a literary work you may actually come across some of these interesting pieces of language in your reading. Here are just a few:

Idiom	**Literally**	**Meaning**
Il fait un temps de chien.	It's dog weather.	The weather is bad.
avoir le cafard	to have the cockroach	to feel sad, down
couter les yeux de la tête	to cost the eyes of one's head	to be very expensive
mettre son grain de sel	to put in one's grain of salt	to give an unsolicited opinion
faire la grasse matinée	to do a fat morning	to sleep in
appeler un chat un chat	to call a cat a cat	to tell the ugly truth

être à l'ouest	to be in the west	to be out of sorts
sauter du coq à l'âne	to jump from rooster to donkey	to skip from topic to topic
un coup de foudre	a bolt of lightning	love at first sight
jeter l'éponge	to throw the sponge	to give up
s'occuper de ses oignons	to take care of one's onions	to mind your own business
en faire tout un fromage	to make a whole cheese out of it	to make a big deal out of it

Work with it

Read the following situations carefully and decide which idiom the person involved would be most likely to use.

1. Le prof explique une idée abstraite, mais ses élèves n'en comprennent rien.

   Idiom: ____________________

2. Ma meilleure amie se plaint d'une situation, mais je pense que c'est elle qui a tort.

   Idiom: ____________________

3. Ma soeur aimerait sortir ce soir, mais il pleut et il fait très froid.

   Idiom: ____________________

4. Quand mon mari s'est réveillé après avoir fait une sieste, il ne savait plus où il était.

   Idiom: ____________________

5. J'ai une étudiante qui a tendance à radoter en présentant ses recherches.

   Idiom: ____________________

III. Grammar

In this last grammar section, we'll look at a few specific phenomena that can be confusing at first glance. The first of these is causative *faire*, used to describe when one person makes another person do something. The next two are the *ne explétif* and *ne* without *pas*, which are essentially opposites of one another. The *ne explétif* is used when no negation is intended, while the *ne* without *pas* still expresses negation.

A. *Causative construction*

The causative construction is used to denote the assigning of tasks or actions to someone else. For example, "I had my house painted" or "I made my students take a quiz." Notice that in the first of these sentences I did not indicate who is doing the painting, but in the second sentence I specified that the students are taking the quiz. The same distinction is possible in French, but the word *faire* is always used, whereas English can use "have" or "make."

Formation: The causative construction is formed by conjugating the verb *faire* in whichever tense is applicable and adding the infinitive form of the verb that is being done. There are three possibilities for this construction. Consider the differences among these three groups:

Elle fait réparer sa voiture.	She's having her car fixed.
Ils font vendre leur maison.	They're having their house sold.
Nous faisons construire un garage.	We're having a garage built.
Le prof fait écrire les étudiants.	The teacher makes the students write.
Je fais chanter mon mari.	I make my husband sing.
Maman fait manger les enfants.	Mom makes the kids eat.
Le prof fait écrire une composition à ses élèves.	The teacher makes her students write a paper.
Je fais chanter la chanson à mon mari.	I make my husband sing the song.
Maman fait manger les légumes aux enfants.	Mom makes the kids eat the vegetables.

In the first group of sentences, only the recipient of the action of the verb is mentioned. What is being fixed? The car. What is being sold? The house. What is being built? The garage.

In group two, we're introduced to the agent, or the person who has to perform the action. Since the agent is the only object involved in this case, there is no need for a preposition.

Once we move on to the third group, however, the situation changes. Since both the recipient and the agent of the action are mentioned, the preposition *à* is added in order to clarify which one is the agent (this could also be accomplished with the preposition *par*, or "by").

The recipient and agent can both be replaced by object pronouns. In either of the first two groups of sentences, this would be accomplished by using a direct object pronoun (*le, la, les, l'*). In the last set of sentences, there would be a direct object pronoun as well as an indirect object pronoun. Let's go back to a few of these sentences and see these pronouns:

Elle fait réparer sa voiture.	She's having her car fixed.
Elle la fait réparer.	She's having it fixed. (recipient)
Le prof fait écrire les étudiants.	The prof makes the students write.
Le prof les fait écrire.	The prof makes them write. (agent)
Je fais chanter la chanson à mon mari.	I make my husband sing the song.
Je la lui fait chanter.	I make him sing it. (recipient and agent)

Note: In the causative construction, even when a direct object pronoun precedes the verb in the *passé composé*, agreement is not necessary. The three sentences with object pronouns above would therefore look like this:

Elle l'a fait réparer.	She had it fixed.
Le prof les a fait écrire.	The teacher made them write.
Je la lui ai fait chanter.	I made him sing it.

Work with it

A. For each of the sentences below, think about the following questions: What is being done? By whom? Who is making it happen?

1. Elle fait travailler ses employés.

2. Les enfants font faire leurs devoirs à leur copain.

3. Je fais nettoyer la maison deux fois par mois.
4. Nous avons fait peindre la maison par nos enfants.
5. Il fait sortir la poubelle à son fils.
6. Cette chanson fait danser les filles.

B. Now consider these sentences rewritten using object pronouns. Reflect on the words that are replaced and how they would sound in English.

1.	Elle fait travailler ses employés.	Elle les fait travailler.
2.	Les enfants font faire leurs devoirs à leur copain.	Les enfants les lui font faire.
3.	Je fais nettoyer la maison deux fois par mois.	Je la fais nettoyer deux fois par mois.
4.	Nous avons fait peindre la maison par nos enfants.	Nous la leur avons fait peindre.
5.	Il fait sortir la poubelle à son fils.	Il la lui fait sortir.
6.	Cette chanson fait danser les filles.	Cette chanson les fait danser.

C. Finally, translate both versions of sentences #1 and #2 from exercise B.

1. ____________________

2. ____________________

B. When you see ne *without a corresponding* pas

A unique case in French is that you will sometimes see the word *ne* to negate a verb without an accompanying *pas*. This is the case for a small set of verbs and in a few specific situations.

Three verbs that never need the word *pas* are *cesser, oser,* and *pouvoir.* This means that as you read you may come across sentences like these:

Il n'osait contredire la parole de son chef.
He didn't dare contradict the words of his leader.

Vous ne cessez de me déranger avec vos questions!
You don't cease to bother me with your questions!

Elles ne peuvent se souvenir des faits.
They can't remember the facts.

Bouger, daigner, and *manquer* can also be used without the *pas,* although this doesn't occur as frequently as for the verbs above.

Je ne bouge après le dîner.	I don't move after dinner.
Elle ne daigne de nous aider.	She doesn't deign to help us.
Ils ne manquent de nous motiver.	They don't fail to motivate us.

The final verb, *savoir,* is a special case. When it expresses uncertainty (including when it's used in the conditional and with an interrogative word), the *pas* is dropped; however, when it is used to talk about not knowing a fact or how to do something, the *pas* is maintained.

Je ne sais si tu me connais.	I don't know if you know me.
Il ne saurait vous rassurer.	He doesn't know how to reassure you.

but

Je ne sais pas la réponse.	I don't know the answer.
Nous ne savons pas faire du ski.	We don't know how to ski.

Finally, *ne* can be used without *pas* with any verb in "if . . . then" statements, expressions related to time, and questions, as seen below:

Elle travaille demain, si je ne me trompe.	She works tomorrow if I'm not mistaken.
Je n'irai pas si tu n'es d'accord.	I won't go if you're not okay with it.
Il y a deux mois que je ne l'ai vu.	I haven't seen him in two months.
Qui ne voudrait y aller?	Who wouldn't want to go there?

C. The ne explétif

The *ne explétif* is used with certain verbs when there is no negation intended. In this case, the *ne* has no grammatical meaning. Much like the *ne* without *pas* above, the *ne explétif* only happens with certain verbs and phrases. It's very important to distinguish between these two types of *ne* and to know which verbs they happen with, since one will be interpreted as negative and the other will be affirmative.

The *ne explétif* is used with many of the same verbs and conjunctions that trigger subjunctive, especially those expressing fear, doubt, and prevention. It can also be found with certain comparative constructions indicating inequality (less than, worse than, etc).

Je crains qu'il ne vienne.	I fear that he's coming.
Réfléchissez avant que vous n'agissiez.	Think before you act.
Elle a peur qu'il ne soit trop tard.	She's afraid it's too late.
Il fait plus froid que je n'ai pensé.	It's colder that I thought.

Work with it

Given what you now know about the *ne explétif* and the *ne* without *pas*, read the following sentences and decide, based on verb and context, which construction you're seeing.

Ex: Vous n'osez vous approcher du patron ce soir. — *ne explétif* / <u>*ne* without *pas*</u>

1. Elles ont trouvé plus de preuves qu'elles ne l'ont pensé. — *ne explétif* / *ne* without *pas*
2. Nous avons peur qu'il ne le fasse. — *ne explétif* / *ne* without *pas*
3. Il ne cesse de parler de sa nouvelle carrière. — *ne explétif* / *ne* without *pas*
4. Elle ne saurait répondre à la question que tu poses. — *ne explétif* / *ne* without *pas*
5. Avant que tu ne choisisses, cherche plus d'infos. — *ne explétif* / *ne* without *pas*
6. Ma mère ne manque de me critiquer. — *ne explétif* / *ne* without *pas*

IV. Reading and translation

Read the following excerpt from *Micromégas* by Voltaire (1752), and answer the questions below.

> Mais revenons à nos voyageurs. En sortant de Jupiter, ils traversèrent un espace d'environ cent millions de lieues, et ils côtoyèrent la

planète de Mars, qui, comme on sait, est cinq fois plus petite que notre petit globe; ils virent deux lunes qui servent à cette planète, et qui ont échappé aux regards de nos astronomes. Je sais bien que le père Castel écrira, et même assez plaisamment, contre l'existence de ces deux lunes; mais je m'en rapporte à ceux qui raisonnent par analogie. Ces bons philosophes-là savent combien il serait difficile que Mars, qui est si loin du soleil, se passât à moins de deux lunes. Quoi qu'il en soit, nos gens trouvèrent cela si petit, qu'ils craignirent de n'y pas trouver de quoi coucher, et ils passèrent leur chemin comme deux voyageurs qui dédaignent un mauvais cabaret de village, et poussent jusqu'à la ville voisine. Mais le Sirien et son compagnon se repentirent bientôt. Ils allèrent long-temps, et ne trouvèrent rien. Enfin ils aperçurent une petite lueur, c'était la terre; cela fit pitié à des gens qui venaient de Jupiter. Cependant, de peur de se repentir une seconde fois, ils résolurent de débarquer. Ils passèrent sur la queue de la comète, et, trouvant une aurore boréale toute prête, ils se mirent dedans, et arrivèrent à terre sur le bord septentrional de la mer Baltique, le cinq juillet mil sept cent trente-sept, nouveau style.

1 Based on what you've read in this chapter and your intuition, which words strike you as being elevated, or academic, language?
2 What will *le père Castel* disagree with in the travelers' observations?
3 How do the travelers get to Earth, i.e. what is their mode of transportation?
4 Translate the highlighted sentences, and check your answers in the back of the book.

Bibliography

Balzac, H. (1874). *La comédie humaine.* Paris: Ve Adre Houssiaux.

Colette (1922). *La maison de Claudine.*

Comte, A. (1830). *Cours de philosophie positive.* Paris: Rouen Frères.

Descartes, R. (1637). *Discours de la méthode.*

Desmazures, A-C-G. (1890). *L'histoire du chevalier d'Iberville.*

Dumas, A. (1845). *Le comte de Monte-Cristo.*

Flaubert, G. (1877). *Un coeur simple.* Paris: Louis Conard.

France, A. (1908). *Vie de Jeanne d'Arc.* Paris: Calmann-Lévy.

Gide, A. (1912). *Les caves du Vatican.* Paris: Mercure de France.

Gide, A. (1919). *Prétextes: Réflexions sur quelques points de littérature et de morale.* Paris: Mercure de France.

Gourmont, R. (1900). *La culture des idées.* Paris: Mercure de France.

Hugo, V. (1831). *Notre dame de Paris.*

Maupassant, G. (1884). *Clair de lune.*

Maupassant, G. (1890) *L'inutile beauté.* Paris: Des vers.

Montesquieu (1892). *Esprit des lois.* Paris: Librairie Ch. Delagrave.

Proust, M. (1896). *Les plaisirs et les jours.* Paris: Calmann Lévy.

Rachilde (1888). *La marquise de Sade.* Paris: Librairie française.

Sand, G. (1876). *Autour de la table.* Paris: Michel Lévy Frères.

Tocqueville, A. (1848). *De la démocratie en Amerique.* Paris: Pagnerre.

Tocqueville, A. (1856). *L'ancien régime et la révolution.* Paris: Michel Lévy Frères.

Verne, J. (1884). *L'archipel en feu.*

Voltaire (1752). *Micromégas.* Paris: Chez Lefèvre.

Vos, L. (1906). *Entre nous.* Groningen: J. B. Wolters.

Answer key

Chapter 1

Funny French!

"To help you better understand your goldfish: joy, anger, fear, sadness, surprise, death."

Vocabulary

A 1. endroit 2. livre 3. table 4. journal 5. église

B cuisine, chapeau, bonne, pommes, monsieur, docteur, pomme, bout (de ficelle), bras, table, blessé

Grammar

Gender and number

A 1. masc 2. fem 3. fem 4. masc 5. masc 6. masc

B 1. trou 2. cheveu 3. roman 4. manteau 5. seau 6. étudiant

Articles

A 1. les 2. le 3. l' 4. l' 5. les 6. la

B 1. des 2. un 3. un 4. un 5. des 6. une

Prepositions

A à la cuisine, le chapeau, la bonne, des pommes, ce monsieur, ma cuisine, le docteur, une pomme, un bout de ficelle, le bras, de la table, le docteur, ce (pauvre petit) blessé, un bout de ficelle

B de + le/of the day, de + les/of the elements, à + le/at the mall, à + les/at the museums, de + le/of the committee

C du pain, du beurre, du vin, de la quiche lorraine

Reading and translation

1 What to have for dinner tonight

2 Partitive: uncountable foods

3 for dinner, at the butcher's, in front of the window

Chapter 2

Funny French!

"When a friend conjugates a verb wrong: correct his spelling/remain friends."

Vocabulary

Common verbs

A 1. vivre 2. arriver 3. donner 4. ouvrir 5. voir

B 1. veux vivre 2. comptent arriver 3. adore donner 4. dois ouvrir 5. espèrent voir

Avoir and *faire* expressions

1. faire des économies 2. avoir peur 3. il fait froid 4. avoir faim 5. faire le ménage 6. il fait du vent

Question words

1. qui 2. à quelle heure 3. avec qui 4. où 5. quelles

Grammar

Subject pronouns

1. g 2. a 3. i 4. c 5. f 6. b 7. h 8. d 9. e

Present tense

A 1. nous aimons 2. il va 3. vous prenez 4. ils choisissent 5. elle remplit 6. tu fais

B 1. aimer 2. aller 3. prendre 4. choisir 5. remplir 6. faire

Negation

A n'aimons pas, n'est pas, n'ai pas, ne peux pas

B 1. pas du tout/not at all 2. jamais/never 3. rien/nothing 4. aucun/any 5. personne/anyone 6. plus/not anymore

Question formation

A 1. Elle est biologiste, n'est-ce pas? 2. Connais-tu mon frère? 3. Est-ce qu'ils adoptent un chien? 4. Est-ce qu'il a peur des abeilles? 5. Répondez-vous aux questions?

B 1. Où 2. qu 3. Quelle 4. qui 5. Où/Quand 6. Pourquoi 7. Quelle 8. Quand

Reading and translation

1 Present tense: c'est, Julie comprend, la question n'est pas, vous n'avez jamais, ment-il, ça n'est pas, je pense, cela sert, la sereine piété ne répugne pas, l'enfant avise, une photographie (qui la) représente, Vous avez, une petite fille qui n'est pas, peut-il

Questions: Qu'est-ce que c'est que ces machinettes-là? Pourquoi s'offusquerait-elle? Vous n'avez jamais vu des médailles? A quoi donc peut-il vous servir?

Negation: la question n'est pas; vous n'avez jamais vu; ça n'est pas; la sereine piété ne répugne pas; une petite fille qui n'est pas non plus

2 It's not pretty-pretty, but I think that it is of some use; Of what use can it thus be to you?

Chapter 3

Funny French!

"How's it going? It's going. How's it going? It's going. A traditional French conversation"

Vocabulary

Common adjectives

1. b 2. d 3. g 4. h 5. f 6. a 7. e 8. c

Common adverbs

immédiate, actuel, tellement, seule, heureusement, généreux

Grammar

Adjectives

A 1. grosse 2. mauvais 3. fatigué 4. nouvelle 5. heureux 6. vraie

B 1. grand, rouge 2. petite, propre, joli 3. certain, nouvelle 4. petit, triste, belle 5. entière, drôles 6. pauvre, vieille, nouveaux

Adverbs

A tellement, encore, beaucoup, après, entièrement, ainsi, toujours, bien, assez, vraiment, souvent, évidemment, joliment, trop, rarement

B 1. voient souvent/see often 2. très mignons/very cute 3. trop beau/too nice 4. vraiment méchant/really mean 5. parle trop/talks too much

Comparing adjectives

2. les chats/+/les chiens 3. les femmes/=/les hommes 4. elle/+/son frère 5. je/-/mon père

Comparing adverbs

A 1. plus 2. moins 3. moins 4. moins 5. plus

B 1. worse 2. as well as 3. less well than 4. less well than 5. better

Comparing nouns and verbs

1. verb 2. noun 3. noun 4. verb 5. verb 6. noun

Superlatives

A 1. the best memory 2. the worst ideas 3. the best friends 4. the worst landlord

B

Adjectives	Adverbs	Nouns	Verbs
le plus bavard	le plus souvent	le plus d'amis	(joue) le plus
le moins difficile	le plus fréquemment	le plus de confiance	(se plaint) le moins

C The right of man is naturally founded on this principle, that diverse nations must do in times of peace the most good, and in times of war the least evil that is possible.

Reading and translation

1 grande, vilaine, longue, ovale, solide, fidèle, honnête

2 formes

3 It's long, it's oval, it has room for many people. It doesn't speak, it doesn't write. . . . It hides its opinions.

Chapter 4

Funny French!

"What is your main quality? I'm very fast at mental calculations. 23 x 543? 37. That's wrong. Yes, but it's fast."

Vocabulary

Cardinal and ordinal numbers

A 1. f 2. d 3. e 4. b 5. c 6. a 7. g

B 1. cinquième 2. trois 3. deux 4. quatrième 5. cent 6. trentième 7. dix

Demonstrative determiners

	Demonstrative det.	Noun	Gender
1	ce	livre	masculine
2	cette	figurine	feminine
3	ces	cartes	feminine
4	ce	coussin	masculine
5	cet	objet	masculine

Possessive determiners

mon idée, ta compagnie, his/her room, ses clés, notre invité, our house, votre portable, leur passion

Grammar

Cardinal and ordinal numbers

1 We're celebrating our tenth wedding anniversary.

2 Our neighbor's son is eight, and he wants two new basketballs.

3 Did you watch the president's speech tonight?

4 We have two dogs, and I want a third.

Demonstrative determiners

A 1. F/S 2. M/P 3. M/S 4. M/S 5. F/S

B 1. near 2. near 3. far 4. near 5. far

Possessive determiners

A 1. his ideas 2. her father 3. our sister 4. his homework

B 1. mon 2. son 3. notre 4. leurs

Reading and translation

1 trois, cinq, une (lieue) et demie, trois

2 son père/her father, ses voisins/his neighbors, sa femme/his wife, son nom/her name, ses frères/her brothers, ses neveux/her nephews, son mari/her husband

3 Her family, mostly her parents. She has three siblings.

4 In this little village of Domremy/destined for the most singular existence/ One of her brothers was a vicar, the other, a roofer; one of her nephews was a carpenter.

Chapter 5

Funny French!

"I've decided to start my 2020 in February. I consider that January was a free trial month."

Vocabulary

Verbs

1. viennent 2. convient 3. maintiens 4. appartient 5. deviennent 6. obtenons

Adverbs of time

1. Actuellement 2. souvent 3. avant 4. enfin 5. D'abord 6. maintenant

Grammar

The imperfect

A–B

1 I was, I liked/être, aimer

2 was talking, was drawing/parler, dessiner

3 went out/sortir

4 was cooking/cuisiner

5 were/être

6 were always/vouloir

The compound past (*le passé composé*)

A a/avoir and vu/voir, as/avoir and acheté/acheter, sont/être and venues/venir, avez/avoir and eu/avoir, suis/être and tombé/tomber, est/être and née/naître

B 1 n'est pas allée
  2 n'étions pas
  3 n'avez pas
  4 ne jouais pas
  5 ne suis pas sortie

C 1 We finished the project.
  2 He went to his neighbor's house.
  3 Did you go out last night?
  4 She had breakfast.

Narration

Imperfect: était, brillait, souriaient, me sentais, me promenais, marchait, discutions

Compound: ai vu, m'a aperçu, s'est arrêté, a commencé, avons continué, ai dû, s'est dit

Reading and translation

1 An abbot/priest named Marignan.
2 It describes him, his states of being, habitual thoughts/actions.
3 "Pourquoi Dieu a-t-il fait cela?" describes a completed action.
4 He imagined himself to sincerely know God, to penetrate his designs, his will, his intentions. Everything seemed to him created in nature with an absolute and admirable logic.

Chapter 6

Funny French!

"The 4 secrets to happiness: wake up, turn off the alarm, turn to the other side, go back to sleep."

Vocabulary

Common reflexive verbs

1. me dépêcher 2. se raser 3. se reposer 4. me réveiller 5. s'habituer à

Common reciprocal verbs

A 1. se rencontrer 2. s'embrasser 3. se téléphoner 4. se parler

B 1. se disputer 2. se parler 3. se rencontrer 4. s'aimer 5. se quitter

Body parts

1. le nez 2. les mains 3. les pieds 4. les cheveux 5. la jambe

Grammar

Reflexive pronouns

A 1. se, reflexive, present 2. s', reciprocal, present 3. nous, reflexive, past 4. te, reflexive, present 5. se, reciprocal, past

B 1. Nous 2. Tu 3. Vous 4. Il/elle/on 5. Je 6. Ils/elles

Conjugation of pronominal verbs

A 1. me levais 2. se retrouvent 3. nous voyons 4. se reposait 5. se soutient

B 1. d 2. c 3. a 4. f 5. b 6. e

C 4, 2, 5, 1, 6, 3

D 1 I was washing my hair when the telephone rang.

2 Do you wake up every day before your son?

3 She was running in the park when she broke her foot.

Reflexives verbs and passive voice

1 French is spoken here.

2 He's interested in math.

3 This book is read often.

4 Ice cream is eaten in the summer.

5 Our newspaper is selling/sells well.

6 White wine should be drunk cold.

7 How is this word spelled/written?

Reading and translation

1 il s'agit/idiomatic; ils se disputent/reciprocal; se divisent/reciprocal; se rapprochent/reciprocal; ils ne se préparent/reflexive; s'avance/reflexive

2 The French revolution – la révolution française; des alliances secrètes; ils se disputent; la liberté politique; une grande Révolution; les destinées du monde.

3 they know well that the French revolution is a local and fleeting accident/ The English perceive, as through a thick veil, the image of a great revolution that's advancing

Chapter 7

Funny French!

"How do you like your coffee in the morning? Silent."

Vocabulary

Direct object pronouns

A 1. m'/me 2. it/le/la 3. them/les 4. her/la

B 1. l'/le film 2. les/les chiens 3. le/l'ordinateur 4. l'/ta question

Indirect object pronouns

1. leur/them 2. te/you/to you 3. leur/them 4. me/to me 5. lui/to him/to her

Grammar

Placement of object pronouns

A 1. les/them 2. leur/them 3. me/me 4. la/it 5. lui/to him

B 1 Je les voyais souvent.

2 Ils leur donnent de l'argent.

3 Tu me téléphones trop.

4 Nous l'avons choisie.

5 Elle lui parlait tous les jours.

Adverbial pronouns *y* and *en*

A 1. en/de la soupe 2. y/chez mon cousin 3. y/à leurs actions 4. en/de travail à faire 5. y/à la boulangerie

B 1 Will you have some more soup? No, I won't have any.

2 Can he go to my cousin's house? Yes, he can go (there).

Order of multiple pronouns

1 lui/en, à sa mère/de cela

2 y/au supermarché

3 les/leur, les jouets/aux enfants

4 en/de vos souvenirs

5 la/leur, une lettre/à ses enfants

6 les/lui, les devoirs/au prof

7 m'/en, pour toi/du pain

8 vous/l', nous/le livre

Reading and translation

1 *Qu'il ne* ***le*** *crois pas*: the *le* refers to the fact he's dying

Mais s'il ***m'en*** *parle?/Il ne* ***vous en*** *parlera pas/Il ne* ***m'en*** *parlera pas?*: the *en* refers to the fact he's dying, translated as "about it." The *vous* and *m'* refer to who he's talking to: me or you.

. . . *il* ***l'****entendait* ***lui*** *parler* . . . : the *l'* refers to Alexis in the third person and the *lui* refers to his uncle, or "to him."

. . . *que je ne* ***l'****aime pas* . . . : the *l'* refers to the uncle.

2 He's dying – *il doit mourir, parler de la mort.*

3 But, if he talks to me about it?/. . . he will believe that I'm not upset, that I don't love him.

Chapter 8

Funny French!

"Who are we? Students! What do we do? We study! And afterward? We forget everything!"

Vocabulary

Relative pronouns

1. dont 2. pour lesquelles 3. ce que 4. qui 5. au sein duquel 6. ce qui 7. que

Interrogative pronouns

A 1. what/obj 2. whom/obj 3. who/subj 4. what/subj 5. what/obj 6. whom/obj

B 1. le vin 2. fête 3. les invités 4. ces voitures 5. un (nouveau) livre

Grammar

Relative pronouns

1 The city we live close to is often overflowing with tourists.

2 She knows very well what is necessary, but she hesitates anyway.

3 Do you remember the family I was talking to you about?

4 I remember it well. It's the moment (when) I fell in love with him.

5 I really appreciated the humor of the people I talked to at the party last night.

6 What I want to know is how she succeeded in getting her diploma.

Interrogative pronouns

A 1. c 2. a 3. b 4. d

B 1 What are you doing tonight?
2 What makes you happy?
3 Whom did you see last week?
4 Who didn't go there?

C 1. laquelle 2. lesquels 3. lequel

Reading and translation

1 l'homme . . . qui a été le plus remarquable de tous; la vie la plus aventureuse; la destinée la plus glorieuse; qui a joué le rôle le plus éminent; etc.

2 **où**: refers to a moment in time (this time of transition) and says what happened during that time (the colony of Saint-Laurent attained a breadth of dominion almost as vast as Europe).

dont: refers back to the man (l'homme) and says that we must first talk about him.

qui: also refers to the man, and talks about his various exploits (was the most remarkable, had the most adventurous life, played the most eminent role).

où: refers to Saint-Joseph Road and says that's where the office of the factory of Notre Dame cathedral is currently located.

3 one must start by studying some of the men of State/it's the illustrious chevalier of Iberville, of the Le Moyne family/one may say that he had the main part (of the glory).

Chapter 9

Funny French!

"My heart forgets those who offend it, but my conscience makes a list anyway."

Vocabulary

Demonstrative pronouns

1. ce cadeau 2. cette actrice 3. ces chaussures 4. cette image 5. les tableaux

Possessive pronouns

1. la sienne 2. les leurs 3. le nôtre 4. les tiennes 5. la vôtre 6. les miens

Disjunctive pronouns

1. lui/him 2. elle/her 3. toi/you 4. eux-mêmes/themselves 5. moi/me

Grammar

Demonstrative pronouns

A 1. cette association caritative/celle-là 2. ces recettes/celles de mon père 3. ce plat-ci/celui-là 4. ces chemisiers/ceux dans l'autre magasin

B 1. this charity/that one 2. these recipes/those of my father 3. this dish or that one 4. these shirts or the ones in the other store

Possessive pronouns

1. le sien/his 2. le mien/mine 3. les tiennes/yours 4. la sienne/his 5. le leur/theirs

Disjunctive pronouns

A

	Subject pronoun	Object pronoun	Disjunctive pronoun
1	il	lui	nous
2	je	le	moi
3	nous	leur	elle
4	tu	les	toi-même

B 1 He didn't want to talk to him/her about us.

2 We told them that it was *her* coat.

Reading and translation

1 Answers may vary.

2 *Ex*: Le bon sens est = good sense is; chacun pense = each person thinks; ce n'est pas assez = it is not enough; etc.

3 those who are the most difficult to please in every other matter/those who only walk very slowly/those who run

Chapter 10

Funny French!

"As long as my boss pretends to pay me well, I'll pretend to work well."

Vocabulary

Expressions of time

A 1. l'après-demain/le lendemain 2. un an 3. une semaine 4. la veille

B 1. next month 2. the last day 3. Last year 4. the next ten days 5. next year

Grammar

Future

A 1. FP/are going to turn in 2. FS/will have 3. FS/will be 4. FP/are going to walk 5. FP/are going to see

B 1. les, verrons, nous, rendront 2. vas en parler, sera 3. ne parlerai pas 4. ne va pas la voir

C 1 We'll see them when they visit us.

2 Are you going to talk about it with your mom, or will she be reticent?

3 Since I'm anxious, I will not speak at the conference.

4 He's not going to see her, even if she apologizes?

Conditional

A 1 He would not like to sell his house.

2 We would be happy to see you.

3 Could you join us tomorrow?

B 1. b 2. d 3. a 4. e 5. c

C

Future	Conditional	Imperfect
ils auront	vous auriez	tu parlais
je donnerai	tu parlerais	nous faisions
on aura	ils auraient	elle donnait

Reading and translation

1 Fifteen days of vacation to get married. His superior says to take whatever time he needs.

2 He offers to make him captain. Dantès is happy – it says "*les yeux brillants de joie*" or "eyes sparkling with joy."

3 The conditional is used to be polite.

4 You take the time you need./Your intention is to name me captain of the Pharaon?

Chapter 11

Funny French!

"Go ahead, give me whatever ridiculous name. Either way, when you call me I won't come."

Vocabulary

Common impersonal expressions

A 1. e 2. d 3. a 4. c 5. b

B 1. pleut 2. fait du vent 3. fait beau 4. fait froid 5. neige

C 1. e 2. c 3. a 4. f 5. b 6. d

Impersonal expressions, verbs, and conjunctions that trigger the subjunctive

A

Obligation	Doubt	Feelings/judgments
il faut que	douter que	il est triste que
exiger que	il n'est pas certain que	regretter que
il vaut mieux que	il est impossible que	il est surprenant que

B 1 doubt

2 doubt

3 necessity

4 conjunction

Grammar

Imperative

A 1. d 2. e 3. b 4. a 5. c

B 1. Give it back to him/her! 2. Go clean your room! 3. Talk to me about it. 4. Let's watch a movie. 5. Listen to your teacher!

Subjunctive

A soit, aille, sentes

B

	Subjunctive or indicative?	Reason?
1	indicative	we know = certainty
2	subjunctive	doubtful = uncertainty
3	a. indicative b. subjunctive	a. I know = certainty b. it's urgent = necessity
4	subjunctive	thrilled = emotion
5	subjunctive	prefer = imposing preference/will

Reading and translation

1 Because it's imperative, the subject pronoun is missing. The *vous* is the reflexive pronoun. When I look up the infinitive, I should make sure to look at the reflexive version of the verb to find the right definition.

2 One is clearly in a position of authority, since he does as he asks and trembles (*tressaillir*).

3 He suggests that Joseph become his partner, probably because he's good at his job (*c'est un peu à vous que nous devons ces résultats* = it's partly to you that we owe these results).

4 Let's talk about something else/the dividend is one of the best that you've had/I no longer want you to have a salary.

Chapter 12

Funny French!

"My incredible talent is being able to be tired without doing anything."

Vocabulary

A 1. punir 2. rester 3. entendre 4. abolir 5. vendre 6. crier

B 1. he will establish 2. you caught/have caught 3. we succeed/are succeeding 4. she responded/has responded 5. I would warn 6. they will hear 7. you were choosing/used to choose 8. I find 9. you will sell

Grammar

Present participles

A allant, rendons, choisissons, écouter, faisant

B 1. dancing/danser 2. walking/marcher, listening/écoutant 3. doing/fais 4. seeing/voyant 5. doing/faisant 6. moving/déménager

Past participles as adjectives

rafraîchi, gâté, fâché, détendu, passé, effrayé, fatigué

Infinitive constructions

1. s'excuser/apologizing 2. passer/to take 3. ne pas passer/not to spend 4. après s'être rendu compte/after having realized

Reading and translation

1 **Present participles/gerunds**

en se privant = depriving oneself of

en se mettant = starting

ne pouvant être = being unable to be

charmant = charming

Past participles

restreinte = restricted, limited

combinée = combined

peu variées = not very varied

Infinitives

sans avoir = without having

de se créer = to create for oneself

d'être attentive = to be attentive

de savoir (admirablement) écouter = to know how to listen (admirably)

2 Celui

3 tâche, fait

4 . . . attempts to create for himself a limited and combined personality, depriving himself of certain influences . . ./how much that one makes me love the dilettante who, unable to be productive and speak, makes the charming decision to be attentive . . .

Chapter 13

Funny French!

"In school we learn about the simple past, but nothing about the complicated future."

Vocabulary

1. efflanqué 2. affubler 3. apercevoir/ont aperçu 4. ébaudir 5. munir

Grammar

A

-er verbs (9)		-ir/-re verbs (2)	avoir/être/faire (2)
glisser	répliquer	répondre	faire
toucher	simuler	reprendre	être
demeurer	continuer		
murmurer	jeter		
demander			

B Imperfect: marchait, était, brillaient, oscillait, soulevaient

Passé simple: entoura, ralentirent, tournèrent, embrassa, disparut

1 past participle as adjective, "supported"

2 gerund, "dragging"

C 1 She didn't respond (responded nothing), and remained stretched out in the carriage with the air of an irritated queen.

2 Then, without command, they turned to the right.

3 He kissed her one more time. She disappeared in the shadows.

Reading and translation

1 Imperfect: rentrait, était (x2), répondait

Passé simple: se montra, arriva, s'arrêta, palît, monta, mordit, s'approcha, dit, laissa, monta, s'assit, ordonna

2 She is cold to him: sans le regarder, ses lèvres dédaigneuses, etc.

3 Me serait-il permis . . . ? He's addressing her formally to request to come with her.

4 The countess of Mascaret showed up on the front steps just as her husband, who was returning home, arrived under the carriage door./. . . she got into the carriage without looking at him, without even seeming to have noticed him/Without being shocked at the tone with which she was responding to him, he got up and sat next to his wife . . .

Chapter 14

Funny French!

"I'll go get something to eat when I've finished the next level of Candy Crush."

Vocabulary

A 1. auparavant 2. dorénavant/désormais 3. à la fois/en même temps 4. à l'avenir 5. longtemps

B 1 As unemployment increases, the situation becomes precarious.

2 I just saw her in the hallway a little while ago.

3 Once a beautiful, prosperous place, it's now deserted.

Grammar

Pluperfect and *le passé antérieur*

1. nous l'eûmes vu 2. tout eut bien changé 3. ils se furent rendu compte 4. elle n'eut pas tué son oncle 5. je n'eus pas rendu le livre

Future perfect

A 1. SP 2. CA 3. CA 4. HN 5. SP

B 1 He can't find his watch; he must have left it at his friend's house.
2 We will have made croissants when you wake up.
3 My parents will visit us once we've bought a bed.
4 The king assassinated his enemies at the ball.
5 You seem sick; you must have caught a cold.

Conditional perfect

A 1. d 2. e 3. f 4. b 5. a 6. c

B 1. c 2. f 3. a 4. d 5. b 6. e

Past subjunctive

A Look back to the explanation above if you're unsure.

B 1. PS 2. IS 3. IS 4. PS

Reading and translation

1 *Passé simple*: s'ecrièrent, se traduisit, eut

Imperfect subjunctive: tendît, se couvrît

Pluperfect subjunctive: eussent rasé, eût amené

2 of mediocre tonnage, the curvature is accented by rising toward the back, nothing more elegant, etc.

3 They were disappointed and swore. The narrator says they were wrong to yell about the bad luck "*avaient tort de crier à la malchance*" because it's not rare to find precious cargo aboard these vessels "*il n'est pas rare de trouver quelque cargaison précieuse à bord.*"

4 Although the breeze tended to get chilly and the sky was covered with "*échillons*" – a name that the Levantines gave to certain clouds of their sky – the *sacolève* diminished nothing of its sails. It had even kept its flying parrot, that an audacious mariner had certainly brought.

Chapter 15

Funny French!

"When you want to start a debate with someone but you realize it's not worth it."

Vocabulary

Transition words

A ainsi, comme, tandis que, quant à

B 1 ainsi – thus, to cite the most admirable example . . .

2 comme – . . . as being but just one fact . . .

3 tandis que – . . . whereas, on the other hand, . . .

4 quant à – As for determining what these are . . .

Commmon academic vocabulary

1. Considérons 2. Cela va sans dire que 3. En ce qui concerne 4. Je constate que

A few idiomatic expressions

1. jeter l'éponge 2. appeler un chat un chat 3. Il fait un temps de chien 4. être à l'ouest 5. sauter du coq à l'âne

Grammar

Causative construction

A 1 She is making the employees work.

2 The children are making their friend do their homework.

3 I'm having the house cleaned by an unnamed person.

4 We are having the house painted by our children.

5 He is making his son take out the garbage.

6 This song is making the girls dance.

C 1 She makes her employees work./She makes them work.

2 The kids make their friend do their homework./The kids make him do it.

The *ne explétif*

1. ne explétif 2. ne explétif 3. ne without pas 4. ne without pas 5. ne explétif 6. ne without pas

Reading and translation

1 Answers may vary. E.g.: revenons, environ, côtoyèrent, quoi qu'il en soit, dédaignent, aperçurent, cependant

2 That there are two moons astronomers hadn't noticed.

3 On the tail of a comet, inside an aurora borealis.

4 On leaving Jupiter, they crossed a space of approximately one hundred million leagues, and they went alongside Mars, which, as one knows, is five times smaller than our globe./They went for a long time, and found nothing. Finally they caught sight of a small glow, it was Earth.

Index